The Seven Letters to the Seven Churches

By Dr. Chuck Missler

Koinonia House

The Seven Letters to the Seven Churches
© Copyright 2017 Koinonia House Inc.
Published by Koinonia House
P.O. Box D
Coeur d'Alene, ID 83816-0347
www.khouse.org

Author: Dr. Chuck Missler
Editor: Amy Joy

ISBN: 978-1-57821-726-7

All Scripture quotations are from the King James Version
of the Holy Bible.

PRINTED IN THE UNITED STATES OF AMERICA

Table of Contents

Ch. 1: The Birth of the Church 1

Ch. 2: Revelation 7

Ch. 3: The Seven Churches 13
Level 1: Each Literal Church *14*
Level 2: Unto the Churches *15*
Level 3: He that Hath an Ear *16*
Level 4: Prophecy and History *17*
Letter Structure *19*

Ch. 4: To the Church at Ephesus 21
Name Meaning *21*
Historical Church Identity *21*
Ephesus Background *21*
Christ's Letter to Ephesus *25*

Ch. 5: To the Church at Smyrna 35
Name Meaning *35*
Historical Church Identity *35*
Smyrna Background *36*
Christ's Letter to Smyrna *37*
Synagogue of Satan *39*
Ten Days *43*

Ch. 6: To the Church at Pergamos 45
Name Meaning *45*
Historical Church Identity *45*
Pergamos Background *48*
Christ's Letter to Pergamos *50*
Balaam *52*

Ch. 7: To the Church at Thyatira 59
Name Meaning *59*
Historical Church Identity *59*

Thyatira Background *60*

Christ's Letter to Thyatira *61*

Jezebel *63*

The Queen of Heaven *66*

**Ch. 8: A Brief History:
The Medieval Church** **75**

The Papacy *76*

The Struggle for Supremacy *77*

Fall of Rome *78*

Charlemagne *78*

The Isidorian Decretals *79*

The Rule of the Harlots (904-963) *80*

The Descent Continues (1012-1047) . . . *81*

*Golden Age of Papal Power
(1049-1294)* *82*

The Inquisition *82*

The Renaissance Popes *83*

The Reformation Popes and Following *85*

Ch. 9: To the Church at Sardis **89**

Name Meaning *89*

Historical Church Identity *89*

Sardis Background *90*

Christ's Letter to Sardis *92*

Keeping Watch *94*

Appearances versus Truth *98*

The Remnant *100*

Ch. 10: To the Church at Philadelphia . . . **103**

Name Meaning *103*

Historical Church Identity *103*

Philadelphia Background *104*

Christ's Letter to Philadelphia *104*

Period of Tribulation *108*

Our Crown *110*

Ch. 11: To the Church at Laodicea 113
    Name Meaning. *113*
    Historical Church Identity. *113*
    Laodicea Background *113*
    Christ's Letter to Laodicea *115*
    Sin in our Times. *122*

Ch. 12: The Churches: A Summary. 125
    Admonitory Application. *125*
    Personal Application *125*
    Overcomer's Promises *126*
    Prophetic Church Period. *126*

Ch. 13: Seven Kingdom Parables. 129

Ch. 14: The Seven Letters and Us 137
Endnotes. 143
About the Author 147

Chapter 1
The Birth of the Church

And when the day of Pentecost was fully come, they were all with one accord in one place. And suddenly there came a sound from heaven as of a rushing mighty wind, and it filled all the house where they were sitting. And there appeared unto them cloven tongues like as of fire, and it sat upon each of them. And they were all filled with the Holy Ghost, and began to speak with other tongues, as the Spirit gave them utterance.

Acts 2:1-4

The Church was birthed fifty days after Jesus Christ rose from the dead. On Pentecost, the Old Testament feast of Shavuot, the Holy Spirit both alighted and lit up the disciples that were gathered together. Men that had hidden in fear only 50 days before now spoke boldly, moved by the Holy Spirit. As the disciples declared in other tongues the works of God, crowds gathered. The once foot-mouthed Peter became the primary speaker, preaching to a Jerusalem filled with Jews in town for the feast, and Acts 2:41 tells that 3,000 souls were added to their number that day.

That was the beginning. During the next 50 years, the message of the Gospel spread throughout the Holy Land, Turkey, Greece, and Italy despite all opposition. The good news of Jesus' resurrection and His sacrifice for our sins burned westward into Europe and eastward into India and south into Africa. The original disciples of Jesus were beaten, imprisoned, and eventually killed, but the saving power of God continued to move through populations of Jews and Gentiles alike.

There is an interesting scene with Jesus, Peter, and John at the end John's Gospel. Jesus asks Peter three times, "Do you love me?" and three times after Peter's affirmation, Jesus tells him to feed His flock. We see here Peter's opportunity to contradict the three times he denied Jesus during the Lord's trial. After Jesus asks Peter three times to feed His sheep, Jesus speaks and warns Peter that when he is old, he will be bound and martyred.

> *Verily, verily, I say unto thee, When thou wast young, thou girdedst thyself, and walkedst whither thou wouldest: but when thou shalt be old, thou shalt stretch forth thy hands, and another shall gird thee, and carry thee whither thou wouldest not. This spake he, signifying by what death he should glorify God. And when he had spoken this, he saith unto him, Follow me.*
>
> John 21:18-19

"Follow me." Those were the words that began all this in Peter's life. Back when Peter and his brother Andrew were just young fishermen, Jesus called to them and said, "Follow me." He told them He would make them fishers of men, and indeed He did. I'm sure that when they dropped their nets, Peter and Andrew had no appreciation for the great work God would do through their lives because they simply agreed to follow Jesus. They certainly did not suspect that we would know their names here, on the other side of the world, 2000 years later. They probably didn't imagine that they would help change the world for all time.

Yet, at the end of John's Gospel, Peter is disturbed by the news that he will be martyred. He turns around and sees John standing by, and he asks, "What about him?" Jesus doesn't tell them the answer to that question. Instead He says, "What does that matter to you, Peter? Just follow me."

> *Jesus saith unto him, If I will that he tarry till I come, what is that to thee? follow thou me. Then went this saying abroad among the brethren, that that disciple should not die: yet Jesus said not unto him, He shall not die; but, If I will that he tarry till I come, what is that to thee?*
>
> John 21:21-22

John was still quite young when Jesus said those words. He might have been the youngest of all the disciples. It's interesting that while John did not tarry until Christ's return, he did see Christ's return take place - in advance.

John the son of Zebedee lived to be an old man. In his 80s, John was exiled to the Island of Patmos for the Gospel of Jesus Christ. Perhaps he gazed at the clouds every day, wondering, "Is this the day? Will my Lord return today?" Jesus did not come back during John's lifetime, but John was given a gift that went beyond the visions of Isaiah and Ezekiel:[1] John saw the end of the world and the Kingdom of God.

God never leaves Himself without a witness in the Scripture. The Book of Acts only covers about 30 years. It seems strange that God would leave us no comment about the remaining 19 centuries and counting.

I suggest to you that Revelation 2-3 is a continuation of the Book of Acts. In the first chapter of Revelation, John sees the ascended, glorified Jesus Christ in Heaven. In the second and third chapters, Jesus dictates seven letters to John for church bodies in seven cities. Despite the teachings of the apostles and Paul's epistles, which had been circulated among all the Christians, trouble had already crept into the early Church.

We are aware that God has ordained a period of time to accomplish His purposes for the Church. The Church Age that we're in has continued from the Feast of Pentecost through the better part of 2000 years. Jesus gave John letters for seven churches in Asia Minor in the first century, but we also see in those seven churches hints of something more. They appear to represent periods that the Church has gone through during the past two millennia, and they represent things that go on in the hearts of every one of us.

Chapter 2

Revelation

Blessed is he that readeth, and they that hear the words of this prophecy, and keep those things which are written therein: for the time is at hand.

Revelation 1:3

I've been studying Revelation for 40 years, and I've found that I can never read it without making a new discovery. There are many things that make Revelation unique. For one, it's the only book of the Bible that promises a blessing to the reader just for reading it. That's not so minor. No other book in the Bible has the audacity to say, "Read me, I'm special." The longest of the Psalms, Psalm 119, focuses on extolling the Word of God, and it describes the blessings received from the Word of God. However, John promises a blessing to the reader just for reading Revelation.

The word "revelation" is a translation of the Greek word *apokalupsis,* which means "unveiling." It's important to note that the word is not plural, but singular, and it's not the Revelation of John. This book is the unveiling, the revealing of Jesus Christ:

*The Revelation of Jesus Christ, which God
gave unto him, to shew unto his servants
things which must shortly come to pass;
and he sent and signified it by his angel
unto his servant John.*

John 1:1

In Revelation 1:9, John tells us that he had been exiled to the Island of Patmos when he received this vision. Traditionally, Revelation has been dated to about A.D. 96, when John was an older man in his 80s. The church father Irenaeus (A.D. 130-202) tells us in *Against Heresies* that John wrote his apocalypse at the end of the reign of the Emperor Domitian.[2] Irenaeus was the student of John's disciple Polycarp, and he is therefore close enough to the life of John to offer trustworthy information. Eusebius offers confirmation, writing that John returned from his exile in Patmos after Domitian died.[3] The end of Domitian's reign was A.D. 96, giving us a bookend for the date of Revelation.

The revelation of Jesus Christ is not limited to John's book, of course. Jesus spoke through King David in Psalm 40:7, "*Then said I, Lo, I come: in the volume of the book it is written of me.*" The entire Bible is the revelation of Jesus Christ. However, Revelation is a particularly special volume. Christ not only shows John end-times events and dictates to him words for the churches, but Revelation ties up the entire story for us.

When Revelation 1:1 says, *"which God gave unto him…"* who is the *him* there? Jesus Christ. God the Father gave the revelation to Jesus Christ to show unto His servants. We have a taste of the Trinity here.

Remember Mark 13:32:

But of that day and that hour knoweth no man, no, not the angels which are in heaven, neither the Son, but the Father.

There are things the Father knew that were hidden from the Son in His humanity. We have a study, *The Trinity,* that describes the many works - from the creation of the world and humankind to the atonement through the death and resurrection of Christ - that the Bible tells us were accomplished by the Father, the Son, and the Holy Spirit. All three members of the Godhead are described as God, with all the powers of God. Yet, we find other verses that show distinctions between the Father, Son and Holy Spirit. The Father knew when Jesus would return, and Jesus did not. The point is that the Father gave the revelation to Jesus Christ, *"to shew unto his servants things which must shortly come to pass."*

It's important to be aware that the 404 verses of Revelation allude to at least 800 verses from the Old Testament. If we've done our homework, and have a mastery of the Old Testament, there are many things that become clear about Revelation. It's a book full of code, and yet the codes are explained throughout the rest of Scripture. One of the many blessings of this book - if we study it with any diligence at all - is that it takes us into every other book of the Bible. We come away from a study of Revelation with a deep respect for the integrity of the total. We have 66 books, penned by 40 different writers over thousands of years, yet we discover that the Bible is a single integrated message. I suggest that every number, every place name in the original autographs was placed there by the LORD's design.

Chapter 1 of Revelation is an introductory and organizational chapter. It sets up certain identities that are developed throughout the rest of the book.

> *Write the things which thou hast seen, and the things which are, and the things which shall be hereafter;*

Revelation 1:19

The first section of Revelation includes the things which John "*hast seen*" - the past. This is John's vision of the Lord Jesus Christ in chapter 1. When John begins writing the book, this particular chapter is in the past. The second section is John's present, "*the things which are.*" This is what is found in the Letters to the Seven Churches in Revelation 2-3. The things that were going on in the churches was the present at that time and has continued to apply to the present day all throughout the Church Age. "*The things which shall be hereafter*" is the third section. It serves as a partitioning phrase that indicates a change; the final act of Earth will then begin.

Here is the surprise for most people. I believe that the most mysterious, the most practical, the most meaningful part of the entire book is the part that most people skim through - chapters 2 and 3. Everybody wants to get into all the weird stuff that starts in chapter 4. I'm guilty of that, too, but Revelation 4:1 is all the future for us. It's exciting stuff, but it's the future. Chapters 2 and 3 deal with the present - the time of the Church. I don't mean when John was writing; I'm talking about this year, next year — until the time of the Gentiles is ended as Paul foretells in Romans 11:25. We discover that the letters to the seven churches of John's day are also the seven churches of our day.

Chapter 3

The Seven Churches

Jesus addresses churches of seven specific cities in these two chapters: Ephesus, Smyrna, Pergamum, Thyatira, Sardis, Philadelphia, and Laodicea. All seven of these were located in ancient Asa Minor on the western side of present-day Turkey. We have never heard of most of these outside of Revelation. We're familiar with the Ephesians, because Paul wrote them a letter. Whoever heard of Smyrna, Pergamos, or Sardis? Philadelphia is of course not Philadelphia, Pennsylvania, but Philadelphia in ancient Greece.

How many epistles are there in the New Testament? Most people will say there are 21 epistles: 13 signed by Paul, two by Peter, three by John, and three others. However, I suggest that there are 28 epistles in the New Testament, and seven of those are written to the churches in Revelation by the glorified Jesus Christ.

We recognize that these seven letters make a nice set, but why these particular seven churches? There were churches in Jerusalem and Antioch, Galatia and Thessalonica, Iconium and Lystra. There were probably a full four letters written from Paul to Corinth, but it's not included. Why these seven? There were a number of important churches in the first century on which we could put our finger, and they certainly all had issues, positive or negative, that Jesus could have addressed. However, we find that these particular churches, that Jesus chose, serve us with at least four levels of meaning.

Level 1: Each Literal Church

The first level is the obvious one. The churches of Ephesus, Smyrna, Pergamos, Thyatira, Sardis, Philadelphia, and Laodicea were in fact literal churches at that time. Archeologists have discovered a lot about these churches and the aspects of their local lives. Much of this information has nothing to do with the content of Christ's letters to the churches, and some of the details are about as exciting as watching grass grow. The real issue is that these were actual, real churches in the first century. They had valid needs and these letters deal with those valid needs.

I call this the local application.

Each letter is a report card. The letters offer exhortation and advice. They offer encouragement and they offer promises to the churches according to the difficulties they faced in the first century. What's more, I suspect that each of these churches was surprised by what Jesus said. Some were doing much better than they thought, and others were doing much worse than they thought.

Level 2: Unto the Churches

Each letter includes a code phrase. In each letter, Christ says, "*He that hath an ear, let him hear what the Spirit saith unto the churches.*" This indicates that the letters are not merely for the individual church to which it's addressed, else these letters could have been privately communicated and we'd have never known about them. These letters were able to benefit members of all the churches. Whoever had an ear to hear was instructed to pay attention to what the Spirit of Christ was telling these churches, because the principles involved applied to everybody.

I call this the admonitory application.

This admonitory application doesn't just apply to the seven churches named in these passages. We discover that no matter what church we attend, at home or abroad, any church body we attend can be described using elements of these seven. There might be two teaspoons of Smyrna and a teaspoon of Ephesus, or there might be a cup of Laodicea in our church body. We can look for elements of these churches in our own congregations.

One important reality that I glean from these letters is the error that had crept into the early Church by the end of the first century. We can trust the words of the apostles, who were filled with the Spirit of God for the very purpose of spreading the Gospel and building the Church. However, there's a tendency for us as scholars to give honor to the early Church fathers, and we have to be careful. There were some great saints who lived in the early centuries of the Christian Church, but by A.D. 96 we see that a number of churches suffered from significant issues. We can depend on the early Church fathers for historical insight, but not for reliable doctrinal guidance. We know that by the time John wrote down the Book of Revelation, the Church was already in trouble.

Level 3: He that Hath an Ear

Take your right hand. Grab your earlobe. Do you have an ear? When Jesus says in each letter, "*He that hath an ear, let him hear what the Spirit saith unto the churches,*" He is speaking to all of us. The Spirit is speaking to both the individual churches and to all the churches, but every one of us should pay attention.

This is the personal application.

We can see ourselves in one or more of these churches. In our culture, we have a particular problem with staying too busy. We might be dedicated to the truth, dedicated to doing many fine things, but Jesus could easily say to some of us as He did to the church in Ephesus, "Yes. You are doing well, but you've left your first love. You're wrapped up in 'doing church' when you should be wrapped in Me." We also live in a very rich culture. Jesus could say to some of us as He did to the church in Laodicea, "You think you are rich because you have a lot of material possessions, but you don't understand that spiritually, you're poor and blind and naked." We might be a true follower of Christ living among those who do not obey Him, or we might have just a little strength. We can see ourselves in these seven churches.

Level 4: Prophecy and History

There is a fourth possible level that is more controversial and speculative, but which I believe is valid. I believe that these seven letters also lay out the history of the Church in advance. These seven letters describe churches that appear to represent the different periods of Church history during the past 2000 years.

In Luke 4:16-21, Jesus famously presents His mandate by reading from Isaiah 61:1-2a:

> *The Spirit of the Lord GOD is upon me; because the LORD hath anointed me to preach good tidings unto the meek; he hath sent me to bind up the brokenhearted, to proclaim liberty to the captives, and the opening of the prison to them that are bound; To proclaim the acceptable year of the LORD*

What is noteworthy is not just what Jesus reads, but what He does not read. He stops reading at a comma, forgoing the next phrase, "*and the day of vengeance of our God.*" We find Jesus here "dividing" the Word of truth.[4] That comma has lasted nearly 2000 years. There is a gap in prophetic history during that comma, but it's a gap that Revelation 2-3 appears to fill in.

We find other gaps in Scripture. When Jesus entered Jerusalem on Palm Sunday and was crucified days later, He fulfilled the first 69 weeks of the 70 weeks prophesied in Daniel 9:25-26.

Know therefore and understand, that from the going forth of the commandment to restore and to build Jerusalem unto the Messiah the Prince shall be seven weeks, and threescore and two weeks: the street shall be built again, and the wall, even in troublous times.

And after threescore and two weeks shall Messiah be cut off, but not for himself: and the people of the prince that shall come shall destroy the city and the sanctuary; and the end thereof shall be with a flood, and unto the end of the war desolations are determined.

And he shall confirm the covenant with many for one week: and in the midst of the week he shall cause the sacrifice and the oblation to cease, and for the overspreading of abominations he shall make it desolate, even until the consummation, and that determined shall be poured upon the desolate.

Daniel 9:25-27

The Messiah came and was summarily murdered, "*but not for Himself.*" Then, in A.D. 70 Jerusalem and the Temple were destroyed as Gabriel describes in the second part of verse 26. However, nearly two millennia have passed since that fulfillment, and we are still awaiting the arrival of the 70th week described in verse 27. An interval is implied in this prophesy, but there's nothing to tell us how long the interval will last. We are still living in that interval, the gap of time that is filled by the Church Age.

I believe that Revelation 2-3 fills in the gap for us on a prophetic level. We will cover this in more depth in a few chapters.

Letter Structure

As we go through these letters, it's useful to recognize that each letter has seven specific parts:

1) Addressee
2) Title(s) for Jesus
3) Commendation or good news
4) Criticism or bad news
5) Exhortation and admonishment
6) "He that hath an ear"
7) Promise to the overcomer

There are some variations to this list as we go through the letters. We find that two letters have no commendation; nothing good is said about them. That's scary. On the other hand, two letters include no criticism; nothing bad is said about them. That's comforting.

We also find something about the last two parts that I find interesting. In the first three letters, the promise to the overcomer comes after the "*He that hath an ear...*" statement. In the fourth letter, the letter to Thyatira, that order switches. The promise to the overcomer is found in the body of the letter, and the letter ends with "*He that hath an ear...*" as a closure. My premise is that nothing in the Scripture is there by accident. The Scripture in its original form was designed by the Holy Spirit, and I believe every detail is relevant.

Let's now look at each letter, noting each part of its structure.

Chapter 4

To the Church at Ephesus

Unto the angel of the church of Ephesus write; These things saith he that holdeth the seven stars in his right hand, who walketh in the midst of the seven golden candlesticks;

Revelation 2:1

Name Meaning

Ephesus means "desirable."

Historical Church Identity

Ephesus represents the early Church.

Ephesus Background

The city of Ephesus sat on the coast of Asia Minor on the Aegean Sea. It was suburban in its architecture, and its theater seated about 25,000 people. The most outstanding architectural feature in Ephesus was the Temple of Diana, or Artemis, the daughter of Zeus and twin sister of Apollo. We think of Greek mythology as collections of fanciful stories, but the Greeks regarded their gods as real beings and their mythologies as history. The Temple of Artemis in Ephesus was one of the

Seven Wonders of the ancient world, four times larger than the Parthenon in Athens. According to Pliny the Elder (A.D. 23-79), the temple was 425 feet long and 225 feet wide, and it included 127 columns with ionic capitals, each about 60 feet high.[5] The entire structure was built of marble, and Pliny described it as a "wonderful monument of Grecian magnificence, and one that merits our genuine admiration."[6]

Before his final arrest and imprisonment, Paul spent his final years in Asia Minor, and in Ephesus in particular. After Paul's missionary work in Ephesus, many people started to follow Christ. Paul worked the better part of three years in Ephesus preaching and building the Christian community.[7]

Ephesus was a major center for magic arts. Paul made a great impact in the area. In Acts 19:19 we read the Christians in Ephesus decided to burn their books of magic, destroying a pile of materials worth 50,000 pieces of silver. The new Christians did this of their own accord, but it alarmed a silversmith named Demetrius who made his living creating and selling silver statues of the goddess Diana. He warned his fellow artisans that Paul's preaching would ruin their line of work and would bring dishonor on the temple of Diana. This caused a great uproar and near-riot among the people, who gathered in the theater for hours shouting, "*Great is Diana of the Ephesians!*"[8]

The town clerk was able to calm down the crowds, and Paul left Ephesus and journeyed through Macedonia north of Greece, visiting the churches in Berea, Thessalonica, and Philippi. When he returned to Asia Minor, he sailed past Ephesus and landed instead at Miletus. Ephesus had become the center of the missionary operations throughout Asia, but Paul called the elders to meet him at Miletus to avoid delays. Acts 20:16 tells us he wanted to get to Jerusalem in time for Pentecost.

In Acts 20, we find Paul's famous farewell to the Ephesian elders. He is on his way to Jerusalem, where he will begin the rest of his life as a prisoner. The Holy Spirit has repeatedly told Paul that he will find bonds and affliction in Jerusalem, but he is willing to go.[9] He knows that this will be the last time he sees his dear friends. He will certainly miss them, but more importantly, Paul is concerned that they will be deceived and led astray when he can no longer be among them.

> *And now, behold, I know that ye all, among whom I have gone preaching the kingdom of God, shall see my face no more. Wherefore I take you to record this day, that I am pure from the blood of all men. For I have not shunned to declare unto you all the counsel of God. Take heed therefore unto yourselves, and to all the flock, over the which the Holy Ghost hath*

made you overseers, to feed the church of God, which he hath purchased with his own blood. For I know this, that after my departing shall grievous wolves enter in among you, not sparing the flock. Also of your own selves shall men arise, speaking perverse things, to draw away disciples after them. Therefore watch, and remember, that by the space of three years I ceased not to warn every one night and day with tears.

Acts 20:25-31

Here in Acts 20, we find that Paul gives the Ephesian elders a prophecy. Deceivers will both enter from the outside and will rise up from the inside. He's been warning them about this, tearfully, for years. We are in the same boat as the people of Ephesus. We can easily be led astray. There are certainly wolves in our culture, spiritual leaders who twist the truth and draw people after them.

Paul reminds the elders of Ephesus that he declared unto them "*all the counsel of God.*" That is how we can avoid error as well. We have the whole Bible readily available to us in printed, audio, and digital forms. We need to study and know the Bible - the entire counsel of God - and not just our favorite parts. The best way to recognize a lie is to already know the truth, and so we need to have the truth of God's Word stored away in our hearts and minds.

Paul's ministry to the Ephesians took place about A.D. 55-57. His letter to the Ephesians was written from Rome about A.D. 62. More than three decades had passed before John was exiled to the Island of Patmos.

Christ's Letter to Ephesus

Unto the angel of the church of Ephesus write; These things saith he that holdeth the seven stars in his right hand, who walketh in the midst of the seven golden candlesticks;

Revelation 2:1

We see from the first verse that these letters are not written the way that we write letters. In my mind they resemble a military memo, where a "From" and a "To" are blocked out at the very beginning. We tend to sign our letters at the end rather than conveniently announcing ourselves at the start. The writer and addressee are laid out immediately at the beginning of this letter to the church at Ephesus.

The addressee is a little unexpected, however. Here in the first verse of chapter 2, we find Jesus directs His attention to *"the angel"* of the church of Ephesus. We'll discover that each letter is addressed to the *aggelos* of that church. Because the Greek word translated "angel" actually means "messenger," some scholars feel that this word simply refers to the human messengers for those churches. I don't see any problem with that. We can also consider the possibility that an actual heavenly angel is assigned to each church. After all, Daniel 10 indicates that there are mighty warrior angels assigned to protect countries. This is a difference of viewpoint that each of us can resolve for ourselves.

The next part of the address is the church name: Ephesus. Remember when I asked why Jesus chose these specific churches? One answer appears to be in their names. The meaning of the church names turns out to highlight or summarize the contents of each letter. Ephesus means "desirable," and Jesus desires her. In this letter He is calling the church of Ephesus back to Him, back to her first love.

We then find the author, which here is given as two of Jesus' titles. In the first chapter of Revelation we read a string of names for Jesus. As He goes through His letters to the churches, Jesus chooses from them for Himself. In His letter to Ephesus, He is "*he that holdeth the seven stars in his right hand, who walketh in the midst of the seven golden candlesticks.*" These are idioms from Chapter 1. The seven candlesticks represent the churches, and the seven stars represent the angels or messengers of the seven churches. We know this, because Jesus already explained it to us in verse 1:20.

There's an interesting mix of idioms here. On the one hand, He holds the stars in His hand. He's in control. On the other hand, He walks among the churches and He's here among us right now. Those are the idioms presented here in Christ's name for Himself in this letter to Ephesus.

> *I know thy works, and thy labour, and*
> *thy patience, and how thou canst not bear*
> *them which are evil: and thou hast tried*
> *them which say they are apostles,*
> *and are not, and hast found them liars:*
> *And hast borne, and hast patience,*
> *and for my name's sake hast laboured,*
> *and hast not fainted.*

Revelation 2:2-3

He continues with praise for the church of Ephesus; He says, "I know thy works." That phrase occurs in many of these letters. He knows what's going on in each church; He's paying attention. You think you've got a problem in your church? Jesus knows and cares more than you do. The people of Ephesus are on their toes, though. They apparently paid attention to Paul's years of warnings with tears, because they are diligent to watch for deceivers in their midst. They didn't take any nonsense. They kept themselves dedicated to God's Word and didn't allow heresy to creep in. It's been 35 years since Paul's ministry, and they've carefully kept the faith during that time and haven't given up.

However, in verse 4 we find a heavy word: "nevertheless."

Nevertheless I have somewhat against thee,
because thou hast left thy first love.

Revelation 2:4

Imagine the owner of your firm comes into your office and says, "Hey, Joe, you've been doing a great job. I've been watching you, and I appreciate all the hard work you've been doing. I really like the way you handled that problem with the Donner case last week. Nevertheless..." The conversation has been going great, but when that word pops out you suddenly feel you're not getting the promotion you'd been hoping was coming.

Jesus tells the Ephesians that, despite all their diligence, they have managed to leave their first love. This isn't just first in sequential order. It's first in rank, in influence, and honor. They have left their number one love, their top love. They gave all their heart to service of the King, but they had forgotten to delight in the King Himself.

As I travel, I find churches that are just like the church in Ephesus. They are on their toes. Their libraries are full of commentaries and they look up the original Greek during their Bible studies. They have a great deal of head knowledge about the Bible, but I find no real affection as I walk around their church bodies. There isn't any love. There isn't any caring, and it's noticeable. Visitors can walk in and leave without being acknowledged, or they can be greeted with warmth but then summarily dropped. The people within the church don't have that bond of comfort and care for each other that should mark every church that serves Christ. There's something wrong there. The people might be spot-on when it comes to doctrine, but they have overlooked the heart of the matter - the love of Jesus Christ. This is no small failing on the part of the Ephesians, and Jesus addresses it with a serious warning:

> *Remember therefore from whence thou art*
> *fallen, and repent, and do the first works;*
> *or else I will come unto thee quickly, and*
> *will remove thy candlestick out of his place,*
> *except thou repent.*

Revelation 2:5

The candlestick is their witness to the world. It's their light in the darkness. This is not a warning that the people will lose their salvation - that's not what Jesus is saying. However, they will lose their witness to a dying world that needs the love of God. I wonder how many churches fall into that category. They have a formal, proud heritage with outstanding catechisms to teach the children, but they fail to spread the Gospel of Christ. We can enter that church and be confronted with the fact that we're sinners in need of the Savior, but not find the overwhelming love and forgiveness of that Savior because the people don't know that love themselves.

What is it to love Jesus Christ and to know His love? Love is the first named fruit of the spirit in Galatians 5. Paul uses the word *agape*, Greek for unconditional love, twenty times in his epistle to the Ephesians alone. God uses marriage to communicate His most intimate truths. There is love in marriage that has nothing to do with *eros*, or sexual adoration. There is the kind of love where two people just enjoy each other's company. They want to be with each other all the time, and they genuinely care for the welfare of the other. It's the kind of love where one person would give his food or risk his life. It's the kind of love that does dishes and folds laundry just because - just to make the other person's burden a little lighter. It's done with a heart of kindness and not from a sense of obligation. That's the kind of relationship we all want, one with that kind of love. We want to have that kind of personal, close, tender relationship with Christ. We don't realize that He longs to have that kind of relationship with us - one in which we can hear His heartbeat.

What is love? Love is willing to be patient and even suffer for the beloved. Love is kind. Love doesn't envy the good fortune of others, but is glad when they do well! Love isn't proud or boastful. It doesn't behave badly or put itself first. When we love people, we expect the best of them and we stick with them and refuse to give up on them. When we see that kind of love in a church body, we know the Spirit of Christ is there.

My wife Nan wrote a fruitful book called *The Way of Agape* based on her studies of God's love during a time in our lives when I was a woefully negligent husband. Her understanding of God's love, and His work in her, saved our marriage. She came to learn how to allow Christ's love to work through her, even while I was taking her for granted. She became a great blessing in my life and in my walk with Christ, and I didn't deserve her.

The failure of the church of Ephesus is a big deal. Jesus admonishes them to remember what they used to have and to return to that. Remember this: repent, and repeat. He tells them to remember the wonderful love they used to enjoy, repent and turn from their current loveless condition, and repeat the works they did at the beginning.

It has been well over 1,900 years since Jesus spoke this letter to the Ephesian church, and much has happened since that day. Where is the thriving, Spirit-filled church in Ephesus? The silting of the harbor dried up this once-great port on the Aegean Sea. Ancient Ephesus is now an archeological site. If there is a living and active church in Ephesus today, we suspect it's a recent rebirth rather than the grandchild of the original church that bloomed there in the first century. It appears that original lampstand was removed.

After this admonishment, however, Christ then gives the Ephesians another word of encouragement.

> *But this thou hast, that thou hatest the deeds of the Nicolaitans, which I also hate.*
> Revelation 2:6

Who were the Nicolaitans? Some ancient authorities have attempted to identify the Nicolaitans by tying them to various sects that existed in those days, but I've found the arguments thin and unconvincing. I prefer the interpretation that is instead a simple translation. The Greek word *nicao* means to "victor over" and *laos* means "the people." That is, Jesus hates the deeds of those who lord over the people. Remember, Jesus gave us an object lesson in organizational hierarchy in John 13 when he washed the disciples' feet. He grabbed a bowl of water and a towel, and He wiped their feet clean, saying:

> *Ye call me Master and Lord: and ye say well; for so I am. If I then, your Lord and Master, have washed your feet; ye also ought to wash one another's feet. For I have given you an example, that ye should do as I have done to you.*

John 13:13-14

It's important that the political structure of the church does not promote moves for power, because that interferes with the mission of the church. A minister of the church isn't there to be served, but to serve others. A clergy that rules over the laity is not biblical. There were to be elders and leaders in the church, but those leaders were there to serve the people and to train them up in the knowledge of Christ. Any time church leadership lords it over the people, we have a real problem.

He that hath an ear, let him hear what the
Spirit saith unto the churches;

Revelation 2:7a

This is the closing phase that occurs as a structural piece in each of the letters. The phrase, "*he that hath an ear, let him hear*" also appears eight times throughout the Gospels.[10] The fingerprints of the Holy Spirit are all over.

Finally, we have the promise to the overcomer.

To him that overcometh will I give to eat
of the tree of life, which is in the midst of
the paradise of God.

Revelation 2:7b

Not only do ancient cultures all have worldwide flood legends, but they also tend to have a Tree of Life. That's interesting. We can find a Tree of Life in the cultures of the Persians, Arabs, Assyrians, Chinese and the Greeks. The Tree of Life can be found in Hinduism and Norse mythology, beside Christianity and Judaism. Thin echoes of Genesis 3 can be heard in each one.

Here we have the promise to the overcomer, one of the main structural features of each of these letters. This promise alludes back to the Garden of Eden, when Adam and Eve were kicked out of the Garden for disobeying God. They were separated from the Tree of Life, but because of Christ's sacrifice we will be free to eat of it once again. In Revelation 22:2, John sees the Tree of Life in Heaven growing on both sides of the river that flows from the throne of God, and in verse 22:14, Jesus declares that those who obey Him will have access to its fruit. Things will have come full circle.

Chapter 5

To the Church at Smyrna

*And unto the angel of the church in
Smyrna write; These things saith the first
and the last, which was dead, and is alive;*

Revelation 2:8

Name Meaning

The name Smyrna derives from the word
myrrh, one of the city's primary exports in its
heyday.

Myrrh is a perfume often used in burial,
and it only gives off its aroma when it's being
crushed, which is significant. Jesus was given
gold, frankincense and myrrh at His birth, each
with a specific symbolism. The gold represented
Christ's kingship, the frankincense represented
His priesthood, and the myrrh foreshadowed His
death and burial.

Historical Church Identity

Smyrna represents the early persecuted
Church.

Smyrna Background

Today, the third largest city in Turkey is called Izmir, Smyrna of the New Testament. The Greek poet Homer was allegedly born in Smyrna, and Alexander the Great is said to have had a dream that it prospered and became one of the greatest cities of the known world. After he died in the late 4th century B.C., Antigonus and Lysimachus built up and fortified the city, and by the 1st century A.D. Smyrna was no small burg. It served as a center of trade, as a port city with two harbors, and it spread up the slopes of Mount Pagos. An impregnable fortress called the Crown of Smyrna was built on the crest of Mount Pagos. The symbolism of the crown came to represent this walled city, and a crown was minted on its coins.

Smyrna was a center of worship for the god of wine, Dionysus, but the people of Smyrna worshiped a variety of deities. The priests of these gods were called *stephanophori*, because they wore distinctive laurel crowns in public processions. These were not diadems, the crowns of royalty, but the *stephanos*, a crown awarded in honor of an accomplishment. The stephanophori were given a laurel or golden crown at the end of their first year in office. It may have been Smyrna where Caesar worship was instituted, with the crown having such a great significant symbolism in that day.

Christ's Letter to Smyrna

> *And unto the angel of the church in*
> *Smyrna write; These things saith the first*
> *and the last, which was dead, and is alive;*
>
> Revelation 2:8

As He did in His letter to the Ephesians, Jesus begins by addressing the recipients of the letter and then giving His titles as the author. Jesus is the First and the Last. He is clearly the being who was dead and is now alive. These are two interesting titles together, because they tell us that Jesus is both God and man.

Christ's letter to the church of Smyrna is a short one, but it also only offers praise and encouragement. These are abused but faithful ones who serve Christ to the death:

> *I know thy works, and tribulation, and*
> *poverty, (but thou art rich) and I know*
> *the blasphemy of them which say they are*
> *Jews, and are not, but are the synagogue*
> *of Satan. Fear none of those things which*
> *thou shalt suffer: behold, the devil shall*
> *cast some of you into prison, that ye may*
> *be tried; and ye shall have tribulation ten*
> *days: be thou faithful unto death, and I*
> *will give thee a crown of life.*
>
> Revelation 2:9-10

This is a heavy letter. Jesus warns the people of Smyrna that they will be imprisoned and persecuted and killed, and He doesn't say that He will deliver them from these troubles. As the name Smyrna implies, they are those who are crushed to give off perfume. They are those who suffer tribulation and death. Jesus has no critique for the people of Smyrna. His encouragement is that He will give them the crown of life when it's all over.

The Lord is not blind to their suffering. Jesus tells them that He knows all about it. They think that they are in bad shape, but God sees things differently. They live in poverty, but Jesus tells them they are actually rich. He encourages them to boldly face the tribulation before them, and He will reward them for it. This is not the Great Tribulation, but the persecution that Jesus promises in John 16:33 and Paul promises in 2 Timothy 3:12.

Are the Christians of Smyrna perfect? Have they never sinned? Certainly they are imperfect humans, but Jesus adds nothing to the burden they already carry. They are facing heavy troubles and death, and He promises them life after death.

He that hath an ear, let him hear what the Spirit saith unto the churches; He that overcometh shall not be hurt of the second death.

Revelation 2:11

We see here an exchange. They will be killed, but God will give them life. They are tormented in a city that is symbolized by a crown, but He will give them the Crown of Life. While they may have to be faithful unto death, the ultimate and final death will have nothing on them.

The Scriptures mention five different crowns for those who love Jesus Christ:

The Crown	Reference	Who Receives It
Crown of Life	James 1:12	He who endures temptation
Crown of Righteousness	2 Timothy 4:8	Those that love His appearing
Crown of Glory	1 Peter 5:4	Servants & examples to the flock
Crown Incorruptible	1 Corinthians 9:25	He who runs the race well
Crown of Rejoicing	1 Thessalonians 2:19	Those who are saved *are* the crown

In Isaiah 60:6 we find that various nations will bring the Messiah gifts from afar during the Millennium. They bring Him gold and frankincense, but no myrrh. Why no myrrh? Because His death and burial are behind Him. He is the resurrected Lord who has come to serve as our King and Priest.

Synagogue of Satan

There's an interesting phrasing in this letter, "*and I know the blasphemy of them which say they are Jews, and are not.*"

Jesus knows about the blasphemy of the Jews, those who did not recognize their own Messiah when He arrived. Christ's words here in Revelation 2 echo back to John 8, when Jesus calls the Pharisees children of the Devil.

> *They answered and said unto him,*
> *Abraham is our father. Jesus saith unto*
> *them, If ye were Abraham's children, ye*
> *would do the works of Abraham.*
> *But now ye seek to kill me, a man that*
> *hath told you the truth, which I have*
> *heard of God: this did not Abraham.*
> *Ye do the deeds of your father.*
>
> John 8:39-41a

Jesus does a turn on them, declaring that their genes are not what's important. It's their hearts and souls, their decisions, their desires that cut them off as children of God's friend Abraham. They don't behave like Abraham. They behave in manners that reflect the heart of their spiritual father, the ultimate rebel.

> *Then said they to him, We be not born of*
> *fornication; we have one Father, even God.*
> *Jesus said unto them, If God were your*
> *Father, ye would love me: for I proceeded*
> *forth and came from God; neither came I*
> *of myself, but he sent me. Why do ye not*
> *understand my speech? even because ye*
> *cannot hear my word. Ye are of your father*
> *the devil, and the lusts of your father ye*
> *will do. He was a murderer from the*
> *beginning, and abode not in the truth,*

because there is no truth in him. When he
speaketh a lie, he speaketh of his own: for
he is a liar, and the father of it.

John 8:41b-44

Jesus claims to be the voice at the Burning Bush a few verses later in John 8:58, saying, "*Before Abraham was, I am.*" We miss it in the English, but the Pharisees did not. They took up stones to stone Him over it. They were not able to kill Him because it wasn't His time. He set up His execution and He laid down His life in fulfillment of the Scriptures. He is the Creator.

Who are the true Jews? Romans 2 tells us they those who are dedicated to God in their hearts:

For he is not a Jew, which is one
outwardly; neither is that circumcision,
which is outward in the flesh: But he
is a Jew, which is one inwardly; and
circumcision is that of the heart, in the
spirit, and not in the letter; whose praise is
not of men, but of God.

Romans 2:28-29

The Jews of Smyrna are clearly coming against the church of Smyrna in the context of Jesus' letter. Jesus tells the people that He knows about their tribulation, and He knows the blasphemy of those of the synagogue of Satan - those who are Jews genetically, but not spiritually. This does not mean that the Church has replaced Israel, and we need to make that clear. God has promises for the descendants of Israel that are separate from the promises for the Church. Ezekiel 37 and Romans 9-11 hammer home that God still has purposes for the Jewish people. Jesus, John, Peter and Paul were all Jews, and God used the Jews to give the world the Gospel. Jesus is King of the Jews, and when He returns, He will reign on David's throne.

Paul divides the New Testament world into three categories: Jews, Gentiles and the Church. In the first few centuries after Christ's resurrection, the Church became very anti-Semitic. That was tragic for the Jews, because throughout 19 centuries, Jews were slaughtered under the banner of Christ. The crusaders had contests to see how many Jewish babies they could catch on a sword. We can go on and on throughout history, and unless we understand that history, we can't grasp the terror of a Jewish person to "Christianity." The fact that Church history doesn't represent the words or heart or life of Jesus Christ isn't the point. Hitler was a practicing Catholic, and he was never excommunicated. If we look at history from the Jewish point of view, Christianity has brutally persecuted the Jews for nearly two millennia. The anti-Semitism is a tragedy. Only during the past century have large numbers of Christians stepped up to love and defend the Jews and to befriend the reborn state of Israel.

Hal Lindsey's 1989 book *A Road to Holocaust* does not lay the Holocaust in Europe at the feet of Germany, but at the feet of the churches in Europe. When Hitler began collecting and slaughtering Jews, the silent pulpits let it happen. The anti-Semitism was preached from the pulpits, and it went back to the early Church fathers. It was tragic for the Jews, but it was also tragic for the Church because we lost our Jewish roots. Jesus fulfills a multitude of Old Testament prophecies, and it's the background of the Old Testament that tells us why Jesus had to come, and who He was, in the first place.

Ten Days

Jesus tells the church of Smyrna that they will have tribulation for ten days. These are ten periods of time. What does that mean exactly, ten days? There were ten major emperors of Rome that made outright moves against the Christians: Claudius (41-54), Nero (54-68), Domitian (81-96), Trajan (98-117), Marcus Aurelius (161-180), Septimius Severus (193-211), Maximinus Thrax (235-238), Decius (249-251), Valerian (253-260), and Diocletian (284-305). Certain emperors were worse than others, but the 1563 history *Foxe's Book of Martyrs* accounts that five million believers died for Christ during this period of the Roman Empire.

The city of Smyrna became devoted to Caesar worship, and of course the Christians refused to worship the emperors. *The Martyrdom of Polycarp*, written between A.D. 150 and 160, describes the death of Polycarp. In his youth Polycarp had been a disciple of the Apostle John, and John appointed him as Bishop of Smyrna. Polycarp was burned at the stake at the age of 86 because he refused to deny Christ.

Jesus tells the church of Smyrna that those who remain faithful unto death will receive the Crown of Life. We mentioned the various crowns described in Scripture. They might be different crowns, but they also might all be different names for the same crown.

It's interesting to me that the church in Smyrna has persisted throughout the ages. Only the churches of Smyrna and Philadelphia have enjoyed a continuous existence since the first century, and these are the two churches for whom Jesus offered no criticism.

Chapter 6

To the Church at Pergamos

And to the angel of the church in Pergamos write; These things saith he which hath the sharp sword with two edges;

Name Meaning

Pergamos means "height" or "elevation" and it ranked as the first city in Asia Minor for its great splendor. Its buildings were built of white marble, and its acropolis stood 1000 feet above the city.

Its name can also be read as a combination of the two root words *per* and *gamos*. The word *per* means "by" and the word *gamos* means "marriage" as in monogamy or bigamy. In other words, Pergamos can also mean "by marriage."

Historical Church Identity

Pergamos represents the Church married to the World.

Emperor Constantine famously fought the Battle of Milvian Bridge in October of A.D. 312. He told the Christian historian Eusebius that he looked into the sky and saw a vision of the cross emblazoned with the words, "In this sign, conquer." Constantine painted the Christian symbol of the cross on his men's shields, and the next day he won the battle. He credited his victory to the Christian God and declared himself a Christian. Whether his conversion was truly a spiritual rebirth or just a political rationalization is a matter of debate. Earlier in his life he'd also experienced a pagan vision at the Grand Temple of the Sun in Gaul.

While Constantine had declared himself a Christian, he reigned over an empire of pagans. Sol Invictus "Unconquerable Sun" and Jupiter Dolichenus, the god of the heavens, played key roles in the administrations of the previous emperors. The Persian cult of Mithra had also spread throughout the empire.

Syncretism is the practice of mixing two different sets of beliefs. We see the remnants of syncretism in our churches even today. We meet for worship on Sunday because of Emperor Constantine's original dedication to Sol Invictus. When he became a Christian, he consolidated the many forms of sun god worship under the Christian God. On March 7, 321, Constantine introduced civil legislation establishing Sunday as the day of rest:

On the venerable Day of the Sun let the magistrates and people residing in cities rest, and let all workshops be closed. In the country, however, persons engaged in agriculture may freely and lawfully continue their pursuits; because it often happens that another day is not so suitable for grain-sowing or for vine-planting; lest by neglecting the proper moment for such operations the bounty of heaven should be lost.[11]

Politically, Constantine was making a smart move. He had a vast empire to rule, and he could unify largely distinct religious groups under one God. However, these people brought all their pagan sun god ideas to the party - ideas birthed back in Babylon. Thus, we have peculiar traditions that have nothing to do with the Bible's description of Jesus' birth. What does a Christmas tree or a yule log or mistletoe have to do with the nativity of our Savior? What do bunnies and chicks and eggs have to with His death and resurrection? These all go back to practices involved in the ancient cults and fertility religions.

Why do we celebrate Christmas on December 25? This was originally a holiday dedicated to Saturn. Do we worship Saturn on that day anymore? No. We are able to take advantage of the Christmas holidays to talk about Jesus Christ, to spread the Gospel to a dying world. Still, religious mixing took place during the 4th century, because Rome was filled with paganism when Constantine legalized Christianity. Rome was still filled with paganism when Emperor Theodosis designated Christianity the state religion later that century. The pagans still existed under Theodosis and the emperors who came after, but now the people were forced to officially join a religion they didn't necessarily understand or believe.

Pergamos Background

Smyrna was situated north of Ephesus on the western coast of Asia Minor, and Pergamos sat north and inland of Smyrna. Ephesus was the great political center, Smyrna was the great commercial center, and Pergamos was the great religious center. *Pergamos* is the feminine form, and *Pergamum* is the neuter form of the city name, and so we see it as both in some Bibles.

Zeus is said to have been born in Pergamos. The city was famous for its vast library and its beautiful temples erected to Zeus, Athena, Apollo and the god of medicine Asclepius. The Great Altar of Pergamon lorded over the city from its lofty position on the acropolis. It measured 125 x 115 feet and stood nearly 50 feet high, and it can be seen today in the Pergamon Museum in Berlin. Scholars believe Jesus means this great altar when He refers to "Satan's throne."

Our ambulances and medical vehicles today bear the Caduceus, the rod of Asclepius, the symbol of the snake wound around a pole. This picture is still associated with medicine and healing. The symbol of the snake on the pole, however, actually goes back to Moses' brazen serpent in Numbers 21. God had Moses make a fiery brass serpent on a pole, and all who looked at it would be healed. Hezekiah had the brazen serpent destroyed in 2 Kings 18:4, because the people had started to worship it. That symbol had already made its impression on the ancient world, and it got adopted into Greek mythology. Pergamos was a center of medicine, and Asclepius the son of Apollo was an important god of the city. Do we worship Asclepius? No, but we see the symbols of ancient idolatry still with us.

Pergamos was the official site of Caesar worship, echoing the worship of Nimrod who founded the Babylonian religion. Babylon was the fountainhead of all idolatry, and we find that many Greek and Roman gods have their roots in Babylonian equivalents. When Cyrus the Great conquered Babylon, the Babylonian priesthood migrated with the Persians. The Persians were eventually conquered by the Greeks and the Greeks by the Romans. The priesthood always followed the power and the money, and the religious traditions migrated to Rome. The same gods and myths of Babylon took on Persian labels in Pergamos, and they took on Roman or Latin labels in Rome. Ishtar, Astarte, Aphrodite and Venus are all the same goddess in different eras. We find the same themes throughout pagan cultures, and I believe Zechariah 5:7-11 prophesies that this wickedness will once again return to Babylon as the base of a worldwide pagan religion.

Christ's Letter to Pergamos

And to the angel of the church in Pergamos write; These things saith he which hath the sharp sword with two edges;

Revelation 2:12

We can already hear the serious nature of this letter in the title that Christ chooses for Himself. He is wielding a sharp, double-edged sword. In Smyrna, Christ was the One who had died but was alive again, the One who offered hope to all who died in Him. To Pergamos, Christ comes with a sword. What is the sword of the Spirit? It is the Word of God.

For the word of God is quick, and powerful, and sharper than any twoedged sword, piercing even to the dividing asunder of soul and spirit, and of the joints and marrow, and is a discerner of the thoughts and intents of the heart.

Hebrews 4:12

In Pergamos we find a church that has married the world and compromised the Word of God. Jesus speaks to Pergamos as One whose mouth holds a two-edged sword. How many churches have drifted away from teaching the Word of God? The Gospel is about the blood of Christ, God's redemptive plan from Genesis 3 to the end of the world. Yet, how many churches today have become social institutions working for community change rather than Spirit-filled bodies spreading the good news of salvation?

However, the church in Pergamos is not without merit; it's doing some things well, despite its unenviable location under Satan's throne. The persecution that began in the Smyrna period of Church history continued somewhat in Pergamos.

> *I know thy works, and where thou dwellest, even where Satan's seat is: and thou holdest fast my name, and hast not denied my faith, even in those days wherein Antipas was my faithful martyr, who was slain among you, where Satan dwelleth.*

Revelation 2:13

From a spiritual point of view, from the Church point of view, that persecution was healthy. Early Christian apologist Tertullian (A.D. 155-240) famously wrote, "The blood of the martyrs is the seed of the Church."[12] Persecution furthered the kingdom, and Christianity spread throughout the known world. Still, here in Pergamos a transition is being made between pure worship of God through Jesus Christ and impure worship compromised by the infection of idolatry.

The church of Pergamos had some things going for them. Even in the middle of that corrupt, pagan city, the Christians clung to the name of Christ. They remained faithful despite persecution and despite living in Satan's own city. However, some serious problems had also crept in.

What Satan failed to accomplish by persecution, he attempted to do by marriage. We can say that Satan changed tactics. Rather than seeking to destroy the Church from the exterior, he worked to degrade the Church from the interior. He married the Church to the world, and that's the tragedy of the Pergamos church.

> *But I have a few things against thee, because thou hast there them that hold the doctrine of Balaam, who taught Balac to cast a stumblingblock before the children of Israel, to eat things sacrificed unto idols, and to commit fornication. So hast thou also them that hold the doctrine of the Nicolaitans, which thing I hate.*
>
> Revelation 2:14-15

Balaam

In Numbers 22, the Moabites and Midianites are concerned about the size of Israel as it comes through their area. Balak son of Zippor, king of Moab, seeks to have the prophet Balaam speak to the LORD and curse Israel on behalf of Moab. Balaam is a prophet for hire. He asks the LORD about it, and the LORD tells Balaam not to go because Israel is blessed. Well, Balak doesn't give up. He sends his most important officials to Balaam, and they urge him to go with them and curse Israel. This time, God tells Balaam to go, but to only say what He tells Balaam to say. God is angry with Balaam over the whole thing; Balaam's heart is not pure. It's Balaam's talking donkey that saves his life. Balaam warns Balak that he can only speak what the LORD gives him to speak, and he ends up blessing Israel three times over the course of the next two chapters. Each time that Balak urges him to curse the Israelites, Balaam blesses them instead.

However, we find out later that Balaam still sought Israel's harm on behalf of Moab. In Numbers 25, we learn that the women of Moab and Midian tempted the men to come sleep with them. They called the Israelites to join in their sacrifices and eat, and to worship and bow down to the god of Peor. As a result of this, 24,000 Israelites died in a plague, and God told the Israelites to destroy the Midianites. It turns out that Balaam was behind all this. He apparently advised Balak on how to take down the Israelites - by tempting them to sin against the LORD:

> *And Moses said unto them, Have ye saved all the women alive? Behold, these caused the children of Israel, through the counsel of Balaam, to commit trespass against the LORD in the matter of Peor, and there was a plague among the congregation of the LORD.*

Numbers 31:15-16

Of course, God had bigger plans for Israel than Balaam ever realized, and Balaam is treated as a bad guy throughout the Bible. It was God's grace and not the Israelites' righteousness that caused Him to bring them in to the Promised Land.[13] Balaam was summarily killed when the Israelites attacked the Midianites in Numbers 31:8.

Here in Pergamos, we have the same problem as the Israelites had in Numbers 25. There are those in Pergamos leading the people to sin. Pergamos is filled with idolatry, and the Christians are honoring those idols by eating the food that is sacrificed to them. They have a problem with fornication and with lording it over each other. Their hearts are not single toward the Lord, and compromise has weaseled its way into the congregation. Spiritual fornication may have been their true problem as much as anything physical. They were mixing their pure doctrine by whoring after false gods. Paganism had begun to creep into the Church.

In Revelation 2, Jesus warns the church of Pergamos to repent:

> *Repent; or else I will come unto thee*
> *quickly, and will fight against them with*
> *the sword of my mouth.*

Revelation 2:16

Failure isn't necessarily the end. Proverbs 24:16 tells us that a just man falls seven times but gets back up again. We can all mess up. When we do, we must go quickly to God, ask for His forgiveness and the cleansing that comes from Jesus' blood. God wants us forgiven and cleansed. He wants us healed. Repentance is the Christian's bar of soap. Any time we fail, we can claim 1 John 1:9:

If we confess our sins, he is faithful and just to forgive us our sins, and to cleanse us from all unrighteousness.

If they didn't repent, however, they were in trouble. Remember, the sword in Christ's mouth is the Sword of the Spirit, which is the Word of God. The Roman sword was a short sword. It was for close-quarters one-on-one combat. It was only effective by special training, but with that special training Rome conquered the world. We need to be training with our own swords, especially since we have them in abundance.

Constantine ordered the production of 50 Bibles during his reign. This was a big deal then, because the Bibles had to be hand copied. We have the tremendous luxury and privilege of owning two or four or ten different copies of the Bible in our own homes. Yet, so often they just sit on our shelves gathering dust. Our swords are no better to us than our training with them.

Jesus does not say He will take away the candle from Pergamos as He said He would do to Ephesus. He says that He will come fight those false prophets with the sword of His mouth. He will come hammer them with the Word of God. The Church does not have the authority to determine what's right and wrong. All we can do is announce what God has said.

> *He that hath an ear, let him hear what the Spirit saith unto the churches; To him that overcometh will I give to eat of the hidden manna, and will give him a white stone, and in the stone a new name written, which no man knoweth saving he that receiveth it.*

Revelation 2:17

As in the previous two letters, Jesus offers a promise to the overcomer. In fact, He offers two different rewards here. First, He promises the hidden manna, which Asaph calls "angels food" in Psalm 78:25. God fed the Israelites manna 40 years in the desert, and it ceased when Joshua crossed the Jordan.[14] The overcomer will get a chance to eat that manna, and more importantly, the overcomer will never hunger again. God will satisfy every need we have.

Jesus also offers the overcomer a white stone with a new name, a secret name, on it. This promise has different possible meanings of significance. There was also a stone ballot in court cases. Jurors cast either a white or black stone to indicate innocence or guilt. A white stone was given to victors at the games. That's the flavor of Christ's promise here. The people of Pergamos worshiped an Asiatic goddess whose temple symbol was a black meteorite. A white stone contrasts with that stone.

The Bible has many stone references. Most importantly, Jesus is the foundation stone.

> *Therefore thus saith the Lord GOD,*
> *Behold, I lay in Zion for a foundation a*
> *stone, a tried stone, a precious corner stone,*
> *a sure foundation: he that believeth shall*
> *not make haste.*
>
> Isaiah 28:16

> *And are built upon the foundation of the*
> *apostles and prophets, Jesus Christ himself*
> *being the chief corner stone;*
>
> Ephesians 2:20

> *If so be ye have tasted that the Lord is*
> *gracious. To whom coming, as unto a*
> *living stone, disallowed indeed of men,*
> *but chosen of God, and precious, Ye also,*
> *as lively stones, are built up a spiritual*
> *house, an holy priesthood, to offer up*
> *spiritual sacrifices, acceptable to God by*
> *Jesus Christ.*
>
> 1 Peter 2:3-5

> *For behold the stone that I have laid before*
> *Joshua; upon one stone shall be seven eyes:*
> *behold, I will engrave the graving thereof,*

> *saith the LORD of hosts, and I will remove*
> *the iniquity of that land in one day.*
>
> Zechariah 3:9

In this case, the white stone has a new name written on it. Remember Abram got the new name Abraham, father of a multitude. Jacob the deceiver became Israel, because he fought with God and prevailed. Simon became Peter, the rock. We too will be given new names. I suspect that the new names will be unique to each of us.

Chapter 7
To the Church at Thyatira

*And unto the angel of the church in
Thyatira write; These things saith the Son
of God, who hath his eyes like unto a flame
of fire, and his feet are like fine brass;*

Revelation 2:18

Name Meaning

Thyatira means "daughter" or "continual
sacrifice." It is connected to either Jezebel or the
Catholic mass.

Historical Church Identity

Thyatira portrays the medieval Church from
A.D. 600 to 1500. The Babylonian mysticism that
had slunk across the pagan world also infected the
young Roman Catholic Church. Just as we saw
the rod of Asclepius in Pergamos and continuing
into our culture today, we see the ancient symbols
of Babylonian paganism in the Roman Catholic
Church. The two keys of Janus and Cybele still
appear on the Papal arms as symbols of spiritual
authority. The danger to the church at Thyatira
did not arise from the persecutions of imperial

Rome nor from the animosity of Jewish attitudes. It arose from within the church itself.

Thyatira Background

The road from Istanbul to Izmir (Smyrna) crosses through the small town of Akhisar where the important military city of Thyatira once stood. In the time of Christ, the roads from Pergamos, Sardis and Smyrna met at Thyatira. It was an old town that had gone through several name changes. Originally it was the Lydian town of Pelopia. It then became Semiramis, then Euhippia. It was taken by the Persians, then Alexander, and then Alexander's general Lysimachus. After his rival Seleucus I Nicator took the city from Lysimachus, it became part of Syria and was converted into a frontier fortress to guard the way to Pergamos. Nicator named it Thyatira after learning that his daughter had been born.

Thyatira became a well-known center for trade guilds. There was a major textiles industry in Thyatira. The city was known for its dyes, particularly its "purple" (scarlet) which was derived either from the madder-root prolific in the area, or from the murex shellfish. In Acts 16, we meet Lydia, a wealthy sales representative from Thyatira living in Philippi. Lydia's specialty was the coveted purple cloth.

Any craftsman who wanted to pursue a trade was required to obtain membership in one of the trade guilds. The guilds provided specific benefits and took actions to protect their interests.

Each guild was under the patronage of a pagan deity, and all proceedings and feasts commenced with paying homage to the patron god or goddess. The Christian tradesman in Thyatira had a dilemma. They had to join a guild to ply their trade, but in doing so they risked offering honor to pagan gods.

Christ's Letter to Thyatira

This letter to Thyatira is the turning point of the seven letters. Starting with this letter, the promise to the overcomer jumps up before the "*he that hath an ear*" statement. Here we also start hearing references to the Second Coming, which gives us a clue that this church will continue until the return of Christ.

> *And unto the angel of the church in Thyatira write; These things saith the Son of God, who hath his eyes like unto a flame of fire, and his feet are like fine brass;*
>
> Revelation 2:18

"The Son of God." This is the only place in the book of Revelation that this term is used. This title offers a contrast to the Queen of Heaven. Mother-goddess worship goes back to the very beginning of false religion, and we find the prophets speaking against it all throughout the Old Testament.

Jesus chooses frightening idioms here in His address. His eyes are like a flame of fire, and His feet are like fine brass. Fire and brass are Levitical symbols for judgment because brass was an alloy that could sustain heat. Sacrifices were made on the brazen altar in the Tabernacle and Temple. The priests also washed in the bronze laver. It seems that Thyatira is in trouble. She's not wholly without redeeming characteristics, but Jesus is using symbols of judgment and cleansing in His title.

> *I know thy works, and charity, and service,*
> *and faith, and thy patience, and thy*
> *works; and the last to be more than*
> *the first.*

Revelation 2:19

These are some excellent qualities. Jesus is paying attention, and He sees the love and service of the church of Thyatira. These people truly care about others, and they serve whole-heartedly. Not only that, but their good works are greater now than when they first started. They have faith and patience in the Lord, and they're doing some really good things. However, they have a serious defect:

> *Notwithstanding I have a few things*
> *against thee, because thou sufferest that*
> *woman Jezebel, which calleth herself a*
> *prophetess, to teach and to seduce my*
> *servants to commit fornication, and to eat*
> *things sacrificed unto idols. And I gave her*
> *space to repent of her fornication; and she*
> *repented not.*

Revelation 2:20-21

We have the same problem here in Thyatira that we found in Pergamos. Not only are the people falling into the temptation of idolatry and fornication, but they are led into this error by a woman whom Jesus refers to as Jezebel. He's given her time to repent, and she's refused.

Jezebel

To understand this Jezebel reference, we need to return to the Old Testament. Jezebel was the wife of Israel's King Ahab, the daughter of Ethbaal king of the Sidonians. Ahab angered the LORD by leading Israel in idolatry, but it was Jezebel who seems to have been the driving force behind it. She was a powerful, manipulative woman devoted to Baal and Astarte worship, and she led Ahab in every kind of evil. In the King James rendition of 1 Kings 16:32-33, we read that Ahab both built an altar to Baal and "made a grove." The word "grove" here is *Asherah*, another name for the Phoenician goddess Astarte. Jezebel worshiped Baal and Astarte, and she encouraged Ahab to do the same.

In 1 Kings 18, we find that Jezebel has been slaughtering the prophets of the LORD, and a righteous man named Obadiah has hidden 100 prophets in caves to protect them. Ahab appears as an evil but weak king who goes along with his wife in all manner of wickedness. In 1 Kings 21, Ahab wants a certain vineyard, but the owner Naboth refuses to sell. Jezebel takes control of the situation, and she treacherously has Naboth killed so that Ahab can take his vineyard. That's the kind of woman Jezebel is. At the end of 1 Kings 21, Ahab repents and humbles himself before the LORD, but Jezebel never does.

1 Kings 18 gives us the fantastic story of Elijah up on Mount Carmel. Jezebel has been killing the prophets of the LORD, and the people of Israel have waffled between Baal worship and worship of the LORD. Elijah calls Ahab to meet him with his 450 prophets of Baal (plus another 400 prophets of Astarte) up on Mount Carmel. These 850 prophets are not just random religious personnel; they are those who eat at Jezebel's table.[15] They are in her employ. Elijah asks the people to decide whether they will follow the LORD or Baal. He then challenges the prophets of Baal to a little duel. He says that two altars will be built, one for Baal and one for the LORD, and whichever God is the true God will send fire and burn the sacrifice.

The prophets of Baal agree and spend all day shouting and calling and cutting themselves, trying to get Baal to listen. Elijah mocks them saying, "Call louder. Maybe he's talking or sleeping. Maybe he's going to the bathroom." The prophets of Baal keep trying until the time of the evening sacrifice without any success. At this point, it's Elijah's turn. He repairs the broken altar of the LORD and adds the wood and cuts up the meat. He then has barrels of water poured over the altar. He digs a ditch around the altar so that the water can pour off the sacrifice and fill up the ditch. When Elijah calls on the LORD, he doesn't have to jump up and down and cut himself. He prays a simple, straightforward prayer, and God answers with flame from heaven. The LORD's fire not only burns up the sacrifice, but it burns up the wood, the stones, and the water in the trench. This impresses the people, who declare, "The LORD is the one who is God!"

Elijah then has all the prophets of Baal captured and brought down to the Kishon brook, where he kills every one of them.

Of course, Jezebel is livid when she finds out about all this, and she threatens to get Elijah. He runs away down to Beersheba, and then he travels another forty days to Mount Horeb, where he hides in a cave. Elijah's life is not dependent on the will of Jezebel, of course, and she is never able to capture and kill him. In fact, Elijah never dies. He is carried away in a whirlwind in 2 Kings 2.

Here in Thyatira, we find an evil woman who leads the people astray just as the first Jezebel did. She is a self-proclaimed prophetess, and she leads the people into fornication and idolatry. God is not going to turn a blind eye to this.

> *Behold, I will cast her into a bed, and them that commit adultery with her into great tribulation, except they repent of their deeds. And I will kill her children with death; and all the churches shall know that I am he which searcheth the*

reins and hearts: and I will give unto every
one of you according to your works.

Revelation 2:22-23

This church has an explicit warning that those who are following after Jezebel are going into tribulation. It sounds as though they won't repent. Her children will die, and her punishment will serve as a warning to all the churches.

The Queen of Heaven

The worship of Astarte, the Queen of Heaven, is a cult that goes back to ancient Babylon and the worship of Semiramis, the consort of Nimrod and mother of Tammuz. Mother goddess worship has persisted throughout the ages in each new prevailing culture. God ordered the Israelites to cut down the Asherah and destroy the altars and idols of the false gods when they conquered Canaan.[16] However, by Judges 3:7, the Israelites are already falling into idol worship by serving the Baals and the Asherah. In Egypt the goddess was Isis and in Persia she was Ishtar. The Phoenician Astarte became Athena and then Venus. This goddess worship is always condemned by God. In Jeremiah, we find the people dedicated to the Queen of Heaven,[17] and the LORD promises destruction for the people because they refuse to repent.[18]

Bits and pieces of Babylonian paganism managed to enter the early Church, especially after the Church was legitimized by the political power of the day. Persecution had kept the early Christians pure and dedicated solely to Christ. When Christianity became the state religion, the paganism of Rome was able to creep into the Church. Suddenly there was honor and riches to be found in the positions of religious leadership, and men could vie for these positions out of pride and ambition rather than a love for God.

In A.D. 378 the bishop of Rome took the title of Pontifex Maximus, and he married the worship of God and the worship of pagan deities in ways that have never been unraveled since. I would urge Roman Catholics to read the Bible through from cover to cover and note the number of Roman Catholic practices that are not based there. The rights, the titles, the vestments, the celibate priests, crucifix worship, the adoration of the Communion "host," the doctrine of transubstantiation, and papal infallibility all have their roots back in the institutionalization of Christianity mixed with pagan practices. The lack of immediate punishment on God's part should not be mistaken for laxity.

Many Catholics venerate Mary as the mother of Jesus, after Gabriel's words in the Luke 1: "*Hail, thou that art highly favoured, the Lord is with thee: blessed art thou among women.*" Mary was greatly favored and she had the honor of giving birth to the Savior of the world and raising Him from a baby. It's right to honor Mary. However, that honor has been corrupted in many Catholic homes in which Mary is worshiped as the Queen of Heaven. This is not biblical, and it smells dangerously of mother-goddess worship from Babylon, which God completely condemns.

Mary was not sinless. Luke 1:47 tells us that Mary had need of a Savior too. All generations will call Mary blessed, but 1 Timothy 2:5 tells us we have only one mediator between God and man, and that's the Lord Jesus Christ. No place in Scripture encourages us to pray to Mary, and it's dangerous and foolish to do so. Jesus sees us. He knows our needs, and He loves us. Even if Mary could hear us, which we can't guarantee, we don't need her to plead to Jesus for us. He knows our needs. We are also not encouraged to seek the help of saints who have passed away. Anytime the Bible speaks of the saints, it is referring to the children of God who live among us. We would be better going to the saints we know can hear, the ones who live next door to us, and asking them to join us in prayer. Praying to Mary is not biblical. Praying with our friends and family and neighbors - that is absolutely biblical.

> *Again I say unto you, That if two of you shall agree on earth as touching any thing that they shall ask, it shall be done for them of my Father which is in heaven. For where two or three are gathered together in my name, there am I in the midst of them.*

Matthew 18:19-20

God is all-powerful. He can see every one of us. He can hear our prayers. He knows the number of hairs on our heads. He sent His Son to die for us! We are valuable to Him!

> *But even the very hairs of your head are all numbered. Fear not therefore: ye are of more value than many sparrows.*
>
> Luke 12:7

It's an insult to God to pray to angels or Mary or dead saints, as though they are more capable than God or care more about us than God, or are paying attention when God is not. The only One we need on our side is Jesus Christ Himself.

Dave Hunt's book *A Woman Rides the Beast*[19] offers the best documentation that I've seen linking the practices of ancient Babylon with the Vatican today. I have no desire to offend Catholics; there are plenty of devoted Catholics who love Jesus Christ. However, there is clearly a deep spiritual connection between the Roman Catholic Church and the pagan practices once in use by the Babylonians. On one hand, Hunt's book has a high probability of offending those with a Catholic background, but on the other hand it's led many people to throw off the trappings of a political administration in favor of devotion to Jesus Christ himself.

In Thyatira, there were evils for which there was no remedy. That's why Jesus is calling them out of these practices.

*But unto you I say, and unto the rest
in Thyatira, as many as have not this
doctrine, and which have not known the
depths of Satan, as they speak; I will put
upon you none other burden. But that
which ye have already hold fast till I come.*

Revelation 2:24-25

"*Till I come.*" There is something exciting about Christ's letter to this church; He offers here the first promise in these letters of the Second Coming. This tells us that this church will continue until Christ comes:

Jesus is kind to the churches in these letters. He addresses their biggest issues and does not overwhelm them with a list. He gives the church of Thyatira no other burden than to hold on to what they already have until His Return. Remember, they had some things they were doing well, and Jesus says, "Just keep on keeping on until I come."

*And he that overcometh, and keepeth my
works unto the end, to him will I give
power over the nations:*

Revelation 2:26

We find here for the first time the order of the letter has changed. Starting here with Thyatira and continuing for the final three letters, Jesus gives His promises to the overcomer before finishing with the "He that hath an ear" directive.

First, Jesus tells the churches that if they overcome and keep doing His works until the end, He will give them power over nations. That's interesting. The original Jezebel's goal was power. That was the goal of the popes who sought to rule Europe for themselves. That has always been Satan's goal - power over the nations. When Satan offers us power in this world, it's a lie. We might achieve temporary domination, but it's ultimately meaningless because we'll die and be under God's judgment. Jesus offers us the honest, righteous privilege to rule as kings with Him.

> *And he shall rule them with a rod of iron; as the vessels of a potter shall they be broken to shivers: even as I received of my Father.*

> Revelation 2:27

The Millennial Reign of Christ will be an interesting time because Jesus will reign with a rod of iron. Right now, evil is free to do its worst. We don't know what a world would be like with Satan bound - in which all evil is dealt with immediately. Isaiah tells us that the Root of Jesse will be filled with wisdom and righteousness, and He will slay the wicked with the breath of His lips.[20] Free of evil, the world will be a lovely place:

> *They shall not hurt nor destroy in all my holy mountain: for the earth shall be full of the knowledge of the LORD, as the*

waters cover the sea. And in that day there
shall be a root of Jesse, which shall stand
for an ensign of the people; to it shall the
Gentiles seek: and his rest shall be glorious.

Isaiah 11:9-10

Christ has additional promises for the overcomers in this letter. He will give them power over the nations, and He will also give them the morning star.

And I will give him the morning star.
He that hath an ear, let him hear what
the Spirit saith unto the churches

Revelation 2:28-29

The morning star is the first light of the day the light that shines before dawn. Satan originally had that glory; Lucifer's name in Hebrew is "the shining one" and is associated with the morning star. The morning star is considered the planet Venus, our favorite mother goddess who has received constant worship. We see here again the deception held in contrast with the reality. The real morning star is no evil spirit seeking worship. It is simply that bright and cheerful planetary light given and named by God. Ultimately, the spiritual morning star is Jesus Christ Himself.

We have also a more sure word of prophecy;
whereunto ye do well that ye take heed,
as unto a light that shineth in a dark

place, until the day dawn, and the day star arise in your hearts:

2 Peter 1:19

I Jesus have sent mine angel to testify unto you these things in the churches. I am the root and the offspring of David, and the bright and morning star.

Revelation 22:16

Chapter 8

A Brief History:
The Medieval Church

*The elders which are among you I exhort,
who am also an elder, and a witness of the
sufferings of Christ, and also a partaker of
the glory that shall be revealed: Feed the
flock of God which is among you, taking
the oversight thereof, not by constraint,
but willingly; not for filthy lucre, but of
a ready mind; Neither as being lords over
God's heritage, but being ensamples to
the flock.*

1 Peter 5:1-3

Under persecution, the Church remained tried and pure. Converting to Christianity meant finding eternal salvation and the love of God, but it also meant a life of service. It meant possible abuse and imprisonment and even execution.

After the Church became married to the world, corruption began to creep in. When the Church became connected to the political governance of the empire, its offices became stations of power. The emperor could offer official church positions as political favors to those who did his bidding.

While local ministers might have laid down their lives in God's service to the people, the higher religious leadership grew increasingly degenerate.

The Papacy

The word Pope means "Papa," or "Father." This title originally applied to all Western bishops, but in about A.D. 500 it began to be used solely for the Bishop of Rome. While Peter is traditionally referred to as the first pope, there is no evidence that he ever served as the Bishop of Rome. Peter would never have accepted the title "Papa" at any rate, because Jesus had specifically told His disciples not to let themselves be called Rabbi or Master or Father.[21]

Even in the first century, Peter was concerned that the leadership of the Church could easily be enticed to seek money and power, and he urged the elders to remember they were servants and examples to the flock. We are told by Eusebius that Peter was executed upside down on a cross,[22] but his lifelong purpose had been to lay down his life, feeding the new Christians as Christ had called him to do.[23]

Silvester I (314-335) was Bishop of Rome when Constantine legalized Christianity. Constantine called and presided over the Council of Nicaea (A.D. 325), demonstrating that he already considered himself an authority over the Church. Even at this time, however, the Bishop of Rome had no jurisdiction over other cities. By the end of the century, the bishops of Rome, Constantinople, Antioch, Jerusalem, and Alexandria came to be called "patriarchs;" they were responsible for the Christians within their provinces. The empire divided between Constantinople and Rome in A.D. 395. Antioch, Jerusalem, and Alexandria recognized the leadership of Constantinople at that point. Subsequently, the struggle between Constantinople and Rome began.

The Struggle for Supremacy

The Bishop of Rome Siricius (395-398) saw his opportunity for power and claimed universal jurisdiction over the Church. Unfortunately for him, the Empire divided into East and West shortly after he came to office. Soon, the Western Roman Empire was breaking up under the barbarians.

Leo I (440-461) convinced Emperor Valentinian III to recognize his claim as Primate of All Bishops in 445. In 452 he persuaded Attila the Hun to spare Rome, and three years later he convinced Genseric the Vandal to spare the city. These victories gave him the prestige he needed to clinch his power. Leo I declared himself Lord of the Whole Church and announced that resistance to his authority was a sure path to Hell. Leo I wanted his universal authority recognized, but the multitude of the world's bishops decided at the Ecumenical Council of Chalcedon (451) to equally divide authority over Christendom between the Patriarch of Constantinople and the Bishop of Rome.

Fall of Rome

As the Roman Empire fell to the barbarians, it might seem the Bishop of Rome's power would go with it. In fact, just the opposite took place. Free of civil authority, with plenty of opportunity for forging alliances, the Bishop of Rome had the opportunity to grab the reigns. In the midst of uncertainty, all eyes turned to the religious leadership in Rome.

Gregory I (590-604) is regarded by many as the first Pope, and he served as one of the purest and best of them. He took a leadership role in stabilizing the kings of Europe during a time of anarchy. He cleaned house in the church leadership, removing unworthy bishops and fighting against simony - the sale of church offices. In his personal life he was a good man. If more had been like him, the history of Medieval Christianity would have been a different story.

Charlemagne

Military leader Charles Martel saved Europe from Islam by his victory at the Battle of Tours in 732. His son Pepin was made King of the Franks (a Germanic people occupying western Germany and northern France). Pope Stephen II (752-757) sought Pepin's help in conquering the Lombards, which had pillaged Italy. When Pepin succeeded, he handed over a large part of central Italy to the Pope. This began the Papal States, a time of papal domination that lasted 1100 years until 1870.

Pepin's son Charlemagne reigned 46 years, winning wars and making conquests. His realm included what is now Germany, France, Switzerland, Austria, Hungary, Belgium, and parts of Spain and Italy. Charlemagne and the popes cooperated, and his rule greatly influenced the papacy's rise to a position of world power.

The Isidorian Decretals

Nicholas I (858-867) was the first pope to wear a crown. In 857 a collection of documents appeared, allegedly filled with letters and decrees of 2nd and 3rd century bishops and councils. These documents offered strong validation of the pope's authority, and they were used to elevate his position. These were mostly forgeries by somebody who used the pseudonym Isidore Mercator, and they were called the *Isidorian Decretals*. It took time for these documents to be declared a fraud, but they were used unashamedly in the meanwhile to promote papal power. During this time, Nicholas I excommunicated Photius, Patriarch of Constantinople, who excommunicated him right back. Until 869 all ecumenical councils were held in the Greek language in locations near Constantinople. At this point the East pulled away from the Roman Church altogether.

The Rule of the Harlots (904-963)

Things became dreadful after Nicholas I, and the 200 years until Gregory VII (1073-1085) are called the Midnight of the Dark Ages. This time period was marked by rampant bribery, corruption, immorality, and bloodshed.

The Lombard Liutprand, Bishop of Cremona (920-972), offers a damning chronicle of events that took place under Marozia, the infamous mistress of Pope Sergius III (904-911). Marozia was the daughter of Theophylact, the senator and civil ruler of Rome, but it was her mother Theodora whose name predominates in the annals of Rome from 900 onward. Cardinal Baronius in the 16th century referred to this time as a "pornocracy."[24] Marozia and her mother Theodora controlled several popes, who served as their puppets. Marozia ruled over Rome herself as senatrix from 926-932. She and her mother reportedly brought a stream of lovers through the papal palace, the most strenuous of which were rewarded with a Roman mitre.[25]

Theodora had John X (914-928) brought from his bishopric in Ravena to Rome and named pope for her amorous convenience. John X had Marozia's husband the Duke of Tuscany executed, and Marozia eventually had John X smothered to death. She then raised three popes in quick succession, namely Leo VI (928- 929), Stephen VII (929-931), and her firstborn son John XI (931-936).

Marozia's grandson John XII (955-963) was a completely immoral being. John XII was tried by the Holy Roman Emperor for homicide, perjury, and incest with his two sisters. Edward Gibbon noted of John XII in 1881:

But we read with some surprise, that this worthy grandson of Marozia lived in public adultery with the matrons of Rome; that the Lateran palace was turned into a school for prostitution, and that his rapes of virgins and widows had deterred the female pilgrims from visiting the tomb of St. Peter, lest, in the devout act, they should be violated by his successor.[26]

That "worthy grandson" died at the age of 27 when a woman's enraged husband clocked him in the head with a hammer while catching them in the act of adultery.

The Descent Continues (1012-1047)

During this time, the papacy went to the highest bidder. Benedict IX (1032-1045) was made Pope at 12-years-old through a bargain with Rome's powerful families. Pope Victor III wrote that Benedict IX was guilty of the crimes of "rapes, murders and other unspeakable acts… His life as a pope so vile, so foul, so execrable, that I shudder to think of it."[27] He opened the papal palace to homosexuals and made it a market for male prostitution. His violent anger and murders are just the beginning, and chroniclers constantly avoid describing his sins, summing up his reign by saying he did things too horrible to describe.

Eventually, the people drove Benedict IX out of Rome, but he returned and reclaimed the throne. He then sold the papacy to his godfather Gregory VI (1045-1047) for a weight of 2000 pounds in gold. Even then, he didn't stay away, but returned again to rival other competing popes, filling Rome with hired assassins and corruption. He was found murdered in 1048, his throat slit. His body was dumped in the woods instead of buried.

Golden Age of Papal Power (1049-1294)

Hildebrand heard the cries for reform and led the papacy into its Golden Age (1049-1294). He managed the five papal administrations prior to his own. He then became Gregory VII (1073-1085), and he worked to stamp out the destructive practice of simony, in which bishops and priests purchased their offices from the kings. This of course brought him in conflict with the royal throne of Germany, and devastating wars followed. Gregory VII eventually died in exile, but he had freed the papacy from imperial control.

Over the next several centuries, the papacy continued to be used as an instrument of domination and subjugation rather than as a beacon for the Gospel.

The Inquisition

Pope Innocent III (1198-1216) was the most powerful of all the popes. He claimed to be the "Vicar of Christ" and the "Supreme

Sovereign over the Church and the World," and he demanded complete allegiance to himself. All the monarchs of Europe, and even the Byzantine Empire, obeyed his will. He ordered two of the crusades and condemned both the Magna Carta and the reading of the Bible in the common languages. He declared papal infallibility and instituted the Inquisition. Vast numbers of people were tortured and executed under his direction and that of his successors.

Innocent III instituted the Inquisition, but Pope Gregory IX perfected it. All citizens were required to inform against heretics, and anyone suspected of heresy was vulnerable to be tortured without knowing the name of his accuser. There were no open trials. Once the Inquisitor gave his judgment, the victims were turned over to the civil authorities for imprisonment or execution. The church and state divided up the victims' properties, which offered the church and state the impetus to condemn anybody they wanted. The Inquisition was clearly a diabolical institution, which for 500 years slaughtered multitudes in the name of the Christian Church.

The Renaissance Popes

The Renaissance popes were those that reigned from 1417 to 1517, between the time of the Western Schism and the Protestant Reformation. We find in them a series of criminals, elected by cardinals who were relatives of popes, kings, and the rich families of Europe.

Pius II (1458-1464) was a writer who is famous for having produced erotic literature in his youth. He instructed young men in the art of seducing women, but as a pope he became exceptionally conservative. He insisted in his papal bull *Execrabilis* (1460) that a general council of the Church could not be superior to the pope. The conciliar movement was killed by this bull, which is a shame because it was trying to bring reforms to the Church.

Paul II (1464-1471), wanted to be called "Our Lady of Pity" and would start crying when he didn't get his way.[28] He loved to get dressed up in the most luxurious finery, and he was known as a collector of statues and jewelry, and possibly handsome young men. Exceptionally paranoid, he was criticized for creating unnamed cardinals to increase the number favorable to himself. He permitted frivolities like horse races, but his anti-Semitism was monstrous; he would have Jews run naked for the sport of onlookers. He required Jews to wear yellow handkerchiefs to identify themselves, an indignity later repeated during the Holocaust.

Sixtus IV (1471-1484) built the Sistine Chapel, but he also made the decree that paying money to the church would free souls from Purgatory. He used the papacy to make himself and his family members rich. Vatican insider Stefano Infessura (1440-1500) recorded information about the pope's homosexual liaisons, about which there were many rumors.

Innocent VIII (1484-1492) produced 16 children by married women and engaged in blatant simony. He tried to exterminate the Waldenses and promoted the brutal Spanish Inquisition.

The worst of the Renaissance popes was Alexander VI (1492-1503), who perpetuated and added to the corruption of those who went before him. He gave his illegitimate children high church positions and murdered off those who opposed him.

Corruption had infected every level of leadership in the Roman church. The offices of Pope and cardinals and bishops were filled with evil men who used the church structure to dominate and control the people of Europe.

The Reformation Popes and Following

When the Protestant Reformation began, the members of the Roman Catholic leadership refused to humble themselves and be reformed.

Leo X (1513-1521) had vast wealth from the multitude of church offices he held. He had been made an archbishop at the age of 8 and a cardinal at age 13. He was ultimately an insanely spoiled young man who was permitted to declare that people could only be saved if they did what he said.

The Roman Catholic Church leaders refused to recognize their many sins. Instead, they proceeded to war against and slaughter those who opposed their degenerate governance. On the night of August 24, 1572, 70,000 French Huguenots were massacred under the orders of papist Catherine de

Medici, and the Pope and his cardinals in Rome sang and rejoiced and congratulated each other.

It took another four centuries, until May 21, 1995, for Pope John Paul II to apologize for the slaughter and burnings at the stake during the Protestant Reformation. Yet, unbiblical doctrines produced by corrupt popes continue to be embraced as revealed truth by millions of faithful Catholics.

Martin Luther did not want to split the Church when he nailed his 95 Theses on the castle church door at Wittenberg. He did not intend to tear the Christian world in half. He merely wanted to reform the Church, to return it to Biblical truth. The Word of God tells us that salvation is by grace through faith in the saving blood of Jesus.[29] It is by regeneration of the innermost man by the work of the Holy Spirit.[30] The Roman Catholic Church's abuses were rampant in the Middle Ages, and the Reformation sought to reform the Church and not divide it.

Yet, the Reformation created its own problems. Yes, it did free people from Rome, and yes some Protestant congregations have been filled with passion for God in Jesus Christ. However, after the religious wars were over, many denominational Protestant churches became spiritually empty buildings. They looked good on the outside while they died on the inside.

These four letters finish up Revelation 2, and we move onto the last three letters in chapter 3.

While Jesus had something positive to say to each of these first four churches, we will find that only one of the next three receives a word of praise from Christ.

Chapter 9
To the Church at Sardis

And unto the angel of the church in Sardis write; These things saith he that hath the seven Spirits of God, and the seven stars…

Revelation 3:1a

Name Meaning

The sardius or sardonyx is a brilliant red agate much like our carnelian. In Revelation 4:3 and 21:20, this stone was the 6th foundation of the New Jerusalem. It was also the first stone in the high priest's breastplate in Exodus 28:17; 39:10, and it was the first stone mentioned in the Garden of God in Ezekiel 28:13.

Historical Church Identity

Sardis represents the proud mainline denominational churches who have lost their mooring in the Spirit of Christ. It is the beautiful but dead church, one that looks lovely on the outside but has no life on the inside.

As proud as we are of the saints that gave of themselves so mightily to the truth of the Gospel, the Reformation didn't go far enough. It didn't deal with its anti-Semitism and its bad eschatology.

The mainline Protestant denominations refused to recognize a literal Millennial Reign of Christ. They denied Israel's place in prophecy, claiming that the Church had replaced Israel.

Most importantly, many mainline churches failed to hold onto the life of the Spirit in their ranks. They became Sunday meeting machines that went through the motions but lost the heart of God. They knew the truth that the Bible is the Word of God and that salvation is by faith. Yet, they fell into self-righteousness, looking clean and dignified on the outside while their light to the world flickered and dimmed.

How many churches do we know that are like that? They may or may not teach that Jesus died for our sins, that we are justified by faith in His blood. The people within those churches dress well and look respectable, but they lack the love and grace of God. They are filled with hypocrisy and judgmental attitudes. They behave as though we are saved by outward appearances rather than by a change of the heart.

Sardis Background

Sardis was once one of the greatest cities in the world. Its renown was described by writers like Aeschylus and Thucydides. It was the capital of the ancient Lydian Empire (1200 B.C.) and it sat in a strategic trade location between Pergamos, Smyrna, Ephesus, Philadelphia and Phrygia, by which it became a wealthy city. At its zenith, its king Croesus and its river, Pactolus became proverbial for riches. Its patron deity was the goddess Cybele, (known as Diana in Ephesus) whose son Midas became the famed king of Phrygia who had the golden touch.

Sardis was situated 60 miles northeast of Smyrna. Its acropolis was built on a hill 950 feet above the broad valley of the Hermus at the foot of Mt. Tmolus. It appeared to be impregnable. However, the sheer cliff was clay, and erosion left occasional cracks which could be exploited by those brave enough to climb its face. Its location provided a false confidence, which was reflected in the character of the inhabitants. They had the outward appearance of strength, which made them lazy about keeping watch. This lack of diligence became the downfall of Sardis on more than one occasion.

When besieged by the Persians in 549 B.C., Croesus left the cliffs unguarded on three sides of the city. After two weeks of the siege, Cyrus offered a reward to any man who could find a way of scaling the steep cliffs. Soon after, a young Persian soldier saw a guard of Sardis lose his helmet over the battlements. The guard picked his way down the face of the cliff, retrieved his helmet, and climbed back up - revealing how simple it was to scale. The following night, Hyeroeades and a Persian party climbed the cliff and clambered over the unguarded battlements to take the city.

The people of Sardis still did not learn their lesson. There were several other times the city fell to enemy invaders. Finally, in 214 B.C. the Seleucids repeated the exploit of Hyeroeades, and the city was taken by Antiochus the Great.

Today the ruins of Sert-Kalessi demonstrates nothing of the city's once great glory.

It's interesting that Sardis has nothing good said about it as a whole. There are a few righteous people in Sardis, but there's no praise at the beginning of the letter as there was with the first four. The self-confidence of Sardis has always led to destruction, and that theme continues in the tone of this letter from Christ.

Christ's Letter to Sardis

> *And unto the angel of the church in Sardis write; These things saith he that hath the seven Spirits of God, and the seven stars; I know thy works, that thou hast a name that thou livest, and art dead.*

Revelation 3:1

Who is Jesus to Sardis? We know from Revelation 1:20 that the seven stars are the angels of the churches, but what are the seven spirits of God?

We discover that these letters to the seven churches bring us repeatedly back to Isaiah 11, which describes the coming Messiah. There in verse 2 we find seven spirits listed:

- The Spirit of the LORD
- The Spirit of Wisdom
- The Spirit of Understanding

- The Spirit of Counsel
- The Spirit of Might
- The Spirit of Knowledge
- The Spirit of the Fear of the LORD

This is the Lord who addresses Himself to Sardis, and Sardis is in serious trouble. In contrast to Christ, the church of Sardis is missing the Spirit of God. It is missing His life.

The word "name" is used repeatedly in connection with Sardis. Name, name, name - all the way through this letter. The church of Sardis has a good reputation as a living body, but it's a lie because its people are spiritually dead. They remind us of the Pharisees, whom Jesus called whitewashed tombs. They look good on the outside, but inside they are full of dead men's bones:

> *Woe unto you, scribes and Pharisees,*
> *hypocrites! for ye are like unto whited*
> *sepulchres, which indeed appear beautiful*
> *outward, but are within full of dead men's*
> *bones, and of all uncleanness. Even so ye*
> *also outwardly appear righteous unto men,*
> *but within ye are full of hypocrisy and*
> *iniquity.*

Matthew 23:27-28

This is obviously not a good place to be. They're on the verge of complete death. Yet, we have a hint that there's still a little life yet in Sardis.

*Be watchful, and strengthen the things
which remain, that are ready to die: for
I have not found thy works perfect before
God. Remember therefore how thou hast
received and heard, and hold fast, and
repent. If therefore thou shalt not watch,
I will come on thee as a thief, and thou
shalt not know what hour I will come
upon thee.*

Revelation 3:2-3

The word "perfect" here is better translated "complete." Any pleasing qualities Sardis might have appear to be like the stalk of a dying plant. Jesus does not accuse them of having bad doctrine. He doesn't accuse them of idolatry. He accuses them of looking okay but being dead.

Despite all its dead leaves, though, Sardis has a little life yet. There's a chance that the plant can revive if it's watered, but it's not looking good. Jesus gives them fair warning that they are in trouble and need to repent immediately.

Keeping Watch

It's interesting to note that Jesus says He'll come upon them as a thief if they don't watch. This is our second reference to Christ's coming. Jesus told the church of Thyatira to hold fast until He came. He warns the church of Sardis to be diligent and watch, lest He come upon them unawares. That implies that they'll be expecting Him and won't be surprised if they *do* watch. As Paul tells us, those who are not watching will be unpleasantly surprised, but those who are watching will not:

> *But ye, brethren, are not in darkness,*
> *that that day should overtake you as a*
> *thief. Ye are all the children of light,*
> *and the children of the day: we are not of*
> *the night, nor of darkness. Therefore let*
> *us not sleep, as do others; but let us watch*
> *and be sober.*
>
> 1 Thessalonians 5:4-6

If they don't repent, they will be like the five foolish virgins in Matthew 25:1-13. These five virgins had been waiting for the Bridegroom, but they didn't have enough spiritual oil to keep their lamps lit until He arrived. While they were out buying more oil, the Bridegroom came and ushered the five wise virgins into the marriage, then shut the door. When the foolish virgins returned, they sought to be allowed into the marriage, and the Bridegroom wouldn't open the door to them. He said, "I don't know you."

There are a range of verses that warn us to be vigilant and keep watch:

In the Garden before His crucifixion in Matthew 26:41, Jesus asked His disciples to watch and pray with Him, "*that ye enter not into temptation.*"

In Mark 13:35, Jesus warns us to watch, because we don't know when the Master of the house is returning.

1 Corinthians 16:13, Paul encourages us, "*Watch ye, stand fast in the faith, quit you like men, be strong.*"

He tells Timothy in 2 Timothy 4:5, "*But watch thou in all things, endure afflictions, do the work of an evangelist, make full proof of thy ministry.*"

In 1 Peter 5:8, Peter warns us, "*Be sober, be vigilant; because your adversary the devil, as a roaring lion, walketh about, seeking whom he may devour.*"

These verses treat us like watchmen on a tower, keeping an eye on the countryside below, guarding against enemies who might attack while all the time watching for the return of our Master. These verses call on us to keep paying attention to the spiritual landscape around us.

Jesus tells the church of Sardis to repent. When He tells them to "hold fast," He uses the present imperative, which indicates continuous action. Stay faithful and keep on keeping on. We want to be faithful and wise stewards, and not like the wicked steward appointed a portion with the unbelievers:

> And the Lord said, Who then is that faithful and wise steward, whom his lord shall make ruler over his household, to give them their portion of meat in due season? Blessed is that servant, whom his lord when he cometh shall find so doing. Of a truth I say unto you, that he will make him ruler over all that he hath. But

and if that servant say in his heart, My
lord delayeth his coming; and shall begin
to beat the menservants and maidens, and
to eat and drink, and to be drunken; The
lord of that servant will come in a day
when he looketh not for him, and at an
hour when he is not aware, and will cut
him in sunder, and will appoint him his
portion with the unbelievers.

Luke 12:42-46

We can all think of certain televangelists who have gotten rich on the donations of trusting souls. We can think of churches where the leadership takes advantage of the flock, using them for money and prestige rather than serving them. We can think of churches where the people treat each other with cruelty and callousness in the name of Christ, when they should be on their knees in prayer and seeking to help those in every kind of trouble.

What does it mean to be watching? What does that look like? It doesn't mean we sell our houses and go sit in a field staring at the sky. No. It means that we keep doing with all our hearts whatever work God has set us to doing, keeping our eyes on His purposes. If we're accountants, we're honest and diligent ones. If we're parents, we're dedicated to raising decent, responsible, kind human beings. If we're neighbors, we're considerate, always looking out for the best interests of those around us. We do this continually, avoiding the temptation to be spasmodic Christians. It's not about going through the motions and looking churchy. It's about living lives, humbly and honestly dedicated to Christ. It's about seeing what is really going on and not judging based on appearances.

Appearances versus Truth

Jesus will not judge based on appearances. In John 4, He offered the woman at the well living water. He knew that she had been married five times and was living with a man she hadn't married. He knew her inside and out, He knew all her sins, and He did not reject her. The men in her life had rejected her over and over again, and she had failed over and over, but Jesus offered her living water that would change her life. We need to make judgments according to the Spirit of God and not according to appearances.

In our modern "enlightened" times, the great truths of the Reformation are being lost. We've denied the inerrancy of the Word of God. It used to be that people who didn't believe the Bible at least treated it with respect, but even people who claim to be Christians deny the Bible as God's Word. We no longer teach the depravity of humankind. The common person on the street, even those who claim to be Christians, believe we can get to heaven by being "good people." In our culture we've rejected justification by faith in Christ alone. People believe all roads lead to heaven.

One of the greatest tragedies in our pulpits today is the failure of our Christian leaders to affirm the deity of Jesus Christ. We understand when the world denies Christ's deity, but when the churches themselves deny it, we are in serious trouble.

In our Christian societies we have failed to keep watch, and these dangerous errors have crept in. In the name of love and tolerance, we've allowed destructive ideas to take hold. Those who stand up for the truth of God's Word are shouted down as intolerant bigots.

Jesus says, *"I am the door of the sheep. All that ever came before me are thieves and robbers..."*[31] There was one entrance to the tabernacle. There was one door in the ark of Noah. There was one door to the wedding in Matthew 25. There is no other way to God but through Jesus Christ, and anybody who says otherwise is a thief and a liar.

Loving people with the love of Christ also means standing up for truth. We cannot allow ourselves to fall into legalism, on one hand, and we cannot deny the truth of the Word of God on the other. If we try to fight this fight by our own brilliance, we will fail. We can only do it well by the guidance of the Holy Spirit - the Spirit of knowledge, wisdom, counsel, might, understanding, and the fear of the Lord. We have to have our lamps filled with His oil if we're going to continue to be a light to the world.

Jesus Christ will come as a surprise to those who aren't looking for Him. There will be great joy, though, for those who long for His appearing.[32]

The people of Sardis have a problem because they have forgotten that the Lord they serve is a real Lord, and He is coming back one day to judge the living and the dead. Yet, even in Sardis God has reserved a few individuals who truly love Him.

The Remnant

> *Thou hast a few names even in Sardis which have not defiled their garments; and they shall walk with me in white: for they are worthy.*

Revelation 3:4

It seems even in the darkest of times, God keeps a remnant of true believers for Himself. In 1 Kings 19, Elijah has fled from Jezebel because she threatened to execute him. He's hidden in a cave at Mount Horeb, and he cries out to God that he's alone! Elijah thinks that he is the only one left, and now they want to kill him too! In 1 Kings 19:18 the LORD tells His faithful prophet, "*Yet I have left me seven thousand in Israel, all the knees which have not bowed unto Baal...*" Even in the worst of times and the most terrible of locations, God has His remnant of faithful servants. This is true even of Sardis, the church of whitewashed tombs.

> *He that overcometh, the same shall be clothed in white raiment; and I will not*

*blot out his name out of the book of life,
but I will confess his name before my
Father, and before his angels. He that hath
an ear, let him hear what the Spirit saith
unto the churches.*

Revelation 3:4

Chapter 10
To the Church at Philadelphia

And to the angel of the church in Philadelphia write; These things saith he that is holy, he that is true, he that hath the key of David, he that openeth, and no man shutteth; and shutteth, and no man openeth;

Revelation 3:7

Name Meaning

The name Philadelphia means "city of brotherly love."

Historical Church Identity

Philadelphia represents the Missionary Church. Faithful believers who have obeyed the call of the Spirit to go out around the world to spread the Gospel to every tongue, tribe, and nation. Even secular cartoons portray missionaries trapped in the cannibals' soup pot, because we all recognize that being a missionary can be a dangerous job. These men and women have risked their lives and comfort to take the good news of salvation into every nook and cranny of the globe.

Philadelphia Background

Philadelphia was the youngest of the cities listed in Revelation 2-3. Now known as Alashehir, it was built in the area acquired by Pergamos in 189 B.C. King Eumenes II of Pergamos had a faithful brother who loved him deeply. This Attalus II won the name Philadelphus ("One who loves his brother"), and the city was named after him for his loyalty and affection to his brother the king of Pergamos.

Wine country surrounded Philadelphia, and naturally its primary Greek god was Dionysus, the god of wine. This city sat on the king's post road from Rome and Troas to Pergamos and Sardis and into the interior of Phrygia. It was well situated as a gateway into Asia Minor and it became a convenient center for spreading the Greek language and culture from Greece into the eastern parts of Lydia and Phrygia. It also became an excellent crossroads for spreading the Gospel.

Philadelphia was in an active volcanic area and suffered repeatedly from earthquakes. A major earthquake nearly destroyed the area in A.D. 17, devastating Sardis and ten other cities. The civic and economic disruption continued for decades, and prosperity was never fully regained.

Christ's Letter to Philadelphia

And to the angel of the church in Philadelphia write; These things saith he

> *that is holy, he that is true, he that hath*
> *the key of David, he that openeth, and no*
> *man shutteth; and shutteth, and no man*
> *openeth;*

Revelation 3:7

This is a remarkable set of titles for Christ. He is holy. We know that Jesus is the Holy One.[33] We know that He is true. He is the true God, and He is truth itself.[34] These are easy to comprehend. However, when He says He "hath the key of David," what does that mean?

This is a direct reference to Isaiah 22, in which God sends Isaiah to speak to Shebna the treasurer and warn him that his days are numbered because of his own self-aggrandizement. God is going to replace Shebna with Eliakim. We meet these two characters later in Isaiah 36 when Sennacherib's armies besiege Jerusalem. God tells Shebna:

> *And it shall come to pass in that day,*
> *that I will call my servant Eliakim the son*
> *of Hilkiah: And I will clothe him with*
> *thy robe, and strengthen him with thy*
> *girdle, and I will commit thy government*
> *into his hand: and he shall be a father to*
> *the inhabitants of Jerusalem, and to the*
> *house of Judah. And the key of the house*
> *of David will I lay upon his shoulder; so*
> *he shall open, and none shall shut; and he*
> *shall shut, and none shall open. And I will*

*fasten him as a nail in a sure place; and he
shall be for a glorious throne to his father's
house.*

Isaiah 22:20-23

The key that hung over Eliakim's shoulder
provided him with the power to give access to
the king. He chose when to unlock the door and
whom to let into the king's throne room. This is
not a permanent situation for Eliakim, but it is
a permanent position for Jesus the Son of David.
The government is committed into Jesus' hand as
promised by Scriptures like Isaiah 9:6-7 and Luke
1:32-33, and all authority is given to Him. He has
the power to make things happen according to His
purposes and His will. Whether a door is opened
or locked tight is up to Him.

*I know thy works: behold, I have set before
thee an open door, and no man can shut
it: for thou hast a little strength, and hast
kept my word, and hast not denied my
name.*

Revelation 3:8

Jesus has the authority to open and shut doors,
and He lets the church of Philadelphia know that
they have access to what they need from God.
Philadelphia is a missionary church, and He will
make their path straight, so to speak. They have
kept His Word and they haven't denied His name.

In a time period when there is rampant denial of the inspiration of God's Word, they have believed and followed it.

> *Behold, I will make them of the synagogue*
> *of Satan, which say they are Jews, and are*
> *not, but do lie; behold, I will make them*
> *to come and worship before thy feet,*
> *and to know that I have loved thee.*
>
> Revelation 3:9

This is quite a wonderful promise. Groups of belligerent Jews had caused great trouble for the early Church. Remember, Paul was one of these when he was Saul of Tarsus, going from city to city and throwing the Christians into jail.[35] Jesus saved Paul and made Him an apostle, and we trust that God will touch the hearts of His people Israel in our day as well. As Paul prophesies in Romans 11:26:

> *And so all Israel shall be saved: as it is*
> *written, There shall come out of Sion the*
> *Deliverer, and shall turn away ungodliness*
> *from Jacob:*

The church of Philadelphia is commended simply for being faithful, and because of their faithfulness, the Lord will do big things. He will both protect them and cause the salvation of others through them.

Period of Tribulation

> *Because thou hast kept the word of my*
> *patience, I also will keep thee from the*
> *hour of temptation, which shall come upon*
> *all the world, to try them that dwell upon*
> *the earth.*

Revelation 3:10

What is the word of His patience? I suggest it's the patient waiting for Christ's millennial reign, when He comes to rule on this earth. The Philadelphia church is patiently waiting for Christ, as Paul prays will be the case for the Thessalonians in 2 Thessalonians 3:5. One of the principal truths recovered by the evangelical movements of the 19th century was the Lord's return for His Church. For many years, the denominational churches have taught that Christ's millennial reign is figurative and not literal. They are not expecting Jesus to actually return to rule on earth, and they are not expecting an actual rapture of the Church. Evangelical churches have taken these passages literally and are again anticipating the arrival of Jesus to catch us up to meet Him in the air, "*and so shall we ever be with the Lord.*"[36]

In the meanwhile, there will be a period of temptation or tribulation on the earth, and Christ promises to spare the Philadelphian church from this time. The word "temptation" here is the Greek word *peirasmos,* which has the idea of putting to the test. It can mean trial, temptation, adversity, affliction, trouble, or tribulation. Jeremiah 30:7 calls this period the "time of Jacob's trouble." We see it taking place in Revelation 12:13-17 when the dragon goes to make war on the woman (Israel) and her seed. It's a time that focuses on Israel, but it involves the whole world.

Paul tells us in 1 Thessalonians 5:9 that "*God hath not appointed us to wrath...*" In Revelation 14, we find that God is preparing to pour out His wrath on the earth on those who received the mark of the Beast. The Church is not appointed to wrath, and God's wrath will be poured out on the earth. Here in verse 10 we learn that God will keep the church of Philadelphia from that hour of tribulation that will come upon "them that dwell upon the earth" to try and test them. We don't dwell upon the earth. We are just passing through. We're strangers and sojourners.

Notice that Jesus doesn't tell the church of Philadelphia that He will keep them from all trouble or persecution or tribulation. He is keeping them from this particular time period. Those who spread the Gospel are being persecuted brutally around the world even right now. We think of those in North Korea and China and Burma and Eritrea and Iran and Syria being tormented for the Word of God. We aren't having our houses burned down and our children starved because we are Christians, but there are people in other countries right now facing these things.

(Remember to pray for our persecuted brothers and sister, by the way. Our prayers can bless these precious people from clear across the world, giving them aid and succor and assistance in ways we could never imagine. Please seek the Holy Spirit's guidance and pray daily for the persecuted Church.)

Our Crown

> *Behold, I come quickly: hold that fast*
> *which thou hast, that no man take*
> *thy crown.*

Revelation 3:11

We find an interesting concept in Scripture, "*The first shall be last and the last shall be first.*" Jesus never tells us not to be first. He simply tells us that the way to be first is by being a servant.[37] Those who humble themselves are those who will be exalted.[38] In fact, Paul tells us to strive to be first, to win that *stephanos,* that incorruptible wreathed crown of victory.

> *Know ye not that they which run in a*
> *race run all, but one receiveth the prize?*
> *So run, that ye may obtain. And every*
> *man that striveth for the mastery is*
> *temperate in all things. Now they do it*
> *to obtain a corruptible crown; but we an*
> *incorruptible.*

1 Corinthians 9:24-25

What does it mean to run this race? What does that look like? The author of Hebrews tells us it means keeping our eyes on Jesus, and following after Him as our example.

Wherefore seeing we also are compassed about with so great a cloud of witnesses, let us lay aside every weight, and the sin which doth so easily beset us, and let us run with patience the race that is set before us, Looking unto Jesus the author and finisher of our faith; who for the joy that was set before him endured the cross, despising the shame, and is set down at the right hand of the throne of God.

Hebrews 12:1-2

Jesus says, "Don't let anybody take your crown!"

Him that overcometh will I make a pillar in the temple of my God, and he shall go no more out: and I will write upon him the name of my God, and the name of the city of my God, which is new Jerusalem, which cometh down out of heaven from my God: and I will write upon him my new name. He that hath an ear, let him hear what the Spirit saith unto the churches.

Revelation 3:12-13

When Jesus gives His promises to the overcomer, they are not simply promises to the members of the named church. They are promises to all those who overcome, and they are remarkable promises.

There were two pillars in Solomon's Temple in Jerusalem, and they each had names. The right pillar was called Jachin, which means, "It shall be established," and the left pillar was called Boaz, which means, "In it is strength."[39] Remember also that Philadelphia was an area of strong seismic activity. A pillar that can stand even in great turmoil is a pillar you want holding up the Temple. It is the portrait of somebody stable and permanent. My wife Nan's book, *The Way of Agape,* details the architecture of the Temple and what it really implies spiritually.

In Heaven, the Temple is not made of stones and marble. It is us. We are the Temple of God. We will surround His throne. The overcomers will never have to leave God again. They will be strong and steadfast beings in the living and breathing Temple of the Almighty God. Christ will engrave on those pillars God's name and the name of the new Jerusalem and Christ's new name.

Chapter 11
To the Church at Laodicea

And unto the angel of the church of the Laodiceans write; These things saith the Amen, the faithful and true witness, the beginning of the creation of God;

Revelation 3:14

Name Meaning

Laodicea means "rule of the people."

Historical Church Identity

Laodicea is the wealthy, self-absorbed church of compromise.

Laodicea Background

About 40 miles southeast of Philadelphia, and just a few miles north of Colossae, stood the large and prosperous city of Laodicea. It rested luxuriously on the banks of the river Lycus, a tributary of the Meander. Laodicea didn't have a good location for military defense, so it survived by compromise. It was an old city, dating to 2000 B.C. Its name was changed from Diospolis to Rhoas by the Lydians, and when Antiochus II captured and rebuilt the town in 250 B.C., he named it after his wife Laodice.

Laodicea was a successful commercial and financial center in central Asia Minor, and the remains of its theater, aqueducts, baths, gymnasium and stadium all testify to the wealth it enjoyed in its heyday. According to the Roman historian Tacitus, Laodicea was able to restore itself after a major earthquake without aid from Rome.[40] Cicero held court in Laodicea and did his banking there. Laodicea was known for producing textiles made from high quality black wool and for its famous school of medicine which produced a particular eye salve called "collyrium."

Six miles east of Laodicea stood the city of Hierapolis, which was renowned for its hot springs. Though Laodicea was built on the Lycus, it depended on water piped in from nearby cities Hierapolis and Colossae. The hot springs water from Hierapolis had cooled to a tepid temperature by the time it reached Laodicea, and the cold water from Colossae had warmed to a tepid temperature as it traveled through the aqueduct in the sun, so Laodicea was a city that truly understood lukewarm water.

The church of Laodicea was likely founded by Paul's friend and coworker Epaphras, who also ministered to the people of Colossae.[41] Colossians 2:1 indicates that neither Colossae nor Laodicea were visited by Paul himself, although he certainly joined Epaphras in his zealous prayers for Colossae and Laodicea and Hierapolis.[42] Paul also wrote Laodicea an epistle, which the people of Colossae were instructed to read, even as the people of Laodicea were to read Paul's epistle to the Colossians.[43] Thirty years before Revelation, Paul warned Archippus in Colossians 4:17 to be diligent in the work of the ministry that God had given him to do. There is a tradition that Archippus became the bishop of Laodicea. It may have been his weakness which contributed to the poor spiritual condition of the church there.

Christ's Letter to Laodicea

And unto the angel of the church of the Laodiceans write; These things saith the Amen, the faithful and true witness, the beginning of the creation of God;

Revelation 3:14

He is the Amen, the solid and trustworthy One, perfect and perfected, faithful and true.

The phrase "beginning of the creation of God" can be confusing terminology, as though Christ is merely a created being. That's clearly not His intention, because we know from several verses that Jesus was in the beginning with God the Father and that the worlds were created through Him.[44] When Paul uses the same kind of terminology in Colossians 1:15-16, he refers to Christ as "*…the firstborn of every creature,*" in one breath while declaring in the next, "*For by him were all things created…*" We need to understand that the word translated "beginning" is *arche* from

115

which we get words like archangel and archenemy. It means "highest" or "chief" or "ruler." Jesus is the chief or ruler of the creation of God. His role as the firstborn also places Him in the highest position. He's the one with the authority.

> *I know thy works, that thou art neither cold nor hot: I would thou wert cold or hot. So then because thou art lukewarm, and neither cold nor hot, I will spue thee out of my mouth.*

> Revelation 3:15-16

The Laodiceans were tepid, just like their water. It's natural to enjoy a drink of chilled water, especially on a hot day. These days we have the convenience of water sanitation and freezers full of ice, but in the ancient days, cold water meant safe water. Icy water from a deep well meant water more likely to be clean and safe to drink. The warm water in Laodicea had traveled through aqueducts, but in that day warm water often meant standing water that had the opportunity to bear bacterial cultures and amoebas and insect larvae. Hot water is good and cold water is good, but lukewarm water at just the right temperature can be used to induce vomiting.

Jesus does not want us lukewarm. He does not want us half-hearted about our faith or our walk with Him. If we're spiritually cold, there's a remedy. If we're spiritually hot, then praise God.

However, if we're lukewarm, then we think we're all right, but we're really in a bad place.

When sharp evangelists go onto college campuses, they work to convert the radicals first. Why? Because when radicals come to recognize who Jesus really is, then they fire up the whole campus. Closet nerds need to be saved too, but the passionate radical will quickly reach more people than the shy souls who hide in their rooms. We should all be full of the fire of God, passionate about loving this world in Christ's name.

Laodicea was named after the wife of Syria's Antiochus II, but the name has a meaning of its own: "rule of the people." In other words, this particular church is not looking to Jesus Christ as its leader. It's ruled by popular opinion. This is the user friendly church that compromised to please the culture.

> *Because thou sayest, I am rich, and increased with goods, and have need of nothing; and knowest not that thou art wretched, and miserable, and poor, and blind, and naked:*

> Revelation 3:17

The church in Laodicea thought they were doing okay, because they had money. They were wealthy, and we humans easily make the mistake of assuming that having money means having the blessing of God on our lives. Al Capone had money too, remember. The Pharisees and Sadducees had money. It's great that certain churches are wealthy and able to develop a wide range of church programs. That's great. But, money doesn't represent God's stamp of approval. The church of Laodicea felt at ease because they had their physical needs met, not realizing that they were spiritually wretched. They weren't dead like the church of Sardis, but they were doing badly enough.

Every one of the seven churches had a surprising report card, but probably none greater than the Laodiceans. They thought they had it made. They were the social church, and their membership included all the top executives of the community. Senators and congressmen attended. The heads of corporations provided large tax deductible donations. They didn't understand that Jesus looked at them through a completely different lens.

> *I counsel thee to buy of me gold tried in the fire, that thou mayest be rich; and white raiment, that thou mayest be clothed, and that the shame of thy nakedness do not appear; and anoint thine eyes with eyesalve, that thou mayest see.*

Revelation 3:18

Jesus offers hope to the Laodiceans. It's not over. They have a chance to fix this thing. It's interesting that Jesus consistently uses metaphors that these churches understand. The Laodiceans knew all about gold and rich raiment and eye salve. These were strengths they had; textile manufacture and banking made the city prosperous. Their doctors had developed a renowned eye ointment. Jesus contrasts their versions with His own, however. They specialized in black woolens, and Jesus offers them pure white spiritual raiment. They produced ointment, but He offers them something better than physical sight - He offers the ability to see the truth.

> *As many as I love, I rebuke and chasten:*
> *be zealous therefore, and repent. Behold,*
> *I stand at the door, and knock: if any man*
> *hear my voice, and open the door, I will*
> *come in to him, and will sup with him,*
> *and he with me.*

Revelation 3:19-20

Jesus doesn't hate the Laodiceans. He loves them, and that's why He's sending them this letter to rebuke them. He's giving them a chance to change before it's too late. After His rebuke, He gives them this beautiful picture. He's standing at the door and knocking! He's not hiding from them or driving them like cattle. He offers them this kind and personal promise. If they just open the door to Him, He will come in and enjoy a meal with them. For a lukewarm church, that's a warm and intimate offer from the King of Creation.

Notice something, however. Jesus is not already inside the church of the Laodiceans. He's standing outside, knocking on the door, waiting to be let in. They need to open the door so that He can join them. It's certain that He was once a part of their congregation, but over the years they must have shut Him out - as they chose instead to be ruled by the opinions of the people.

> *To him that overcometh will I grant to sit with me in my throne, even as I also overcame, and am set down with my Father in his throne. He that hath an ear, let him hear what the Spirit saith unto the churches.*

Revelation 3:21-22

We have a great High Priest who passed through the heavens and dwelt with us, taking on the form of a human and living life here with us. He was tempted in all ways just as we are, yet without sin. This gives us great freedom to fall boldly at His throne to seek help in times of need, because He understands exactly what we're going through.[45] He knows. He's been there Himself. He overcame, and that's the greatest news of eternity. Jesus Christ overcame. He conquered!

As we read through these promises to the overcomer, we remember how it is we overcome. We are overcomers through His victory - and His victory in our lives.

*And they overcame him by the blood
of the Lamb, and by the word of their
testimony; and they loved not their lives
unto the death.*

Revelation 12:11

There is an inscription on a cathedral in Lubeck, Germany that I'd like to present here. As we read these letters, we remember that they are written to churches that existed nearly two millennia ago, but they apply to every one of us. We can agree the churches are historical and we can see their prophetic links to churches of the Church Age, but these churches also represent us personally.

- Thus speaketh Christ our Lord to us:
- Ye call Me Master and obey Me not.
- Ye call Me Light and see Me not.
- Ye call Me Way and walk Me not.
- Ye call Me Life and choose Me not.
- Ye call Me Wise and follow Me not.
- Ye call Me Fair and love Me not.
- Ye call Me Rich and ask Me not.
- Ye call Me Eternal and seek Me not.
- Ye call Me Noble and serve Me not.
- Ye call Me Gracious and trust Me not.
- Ye call Me Might and honor Me not.
- Ye call Me Just and fear Me not.
- If I condemn you, blame Me not.

That gets the point across.

Sin in our Times

We believe in liberty in our culture, but it's gotten out of control. There's a point at which we need to agree with God, "No. That's wrong. We don't do that." The world will do what the world does. However, in our churches do we let the culture tell us what to think, or do we follow the Word of God?

Sin is an uncomfortable subject in our times. Our culture no longer believes in sin. Yet, without a recognition of our own personal failure, a recognition that we deserve to be punished, there's no reason for us to seek a Savior. Jesus did not come to condemn us, but to save us. However, without the conviction of our sin, we have no understanding that we need to be saved. We think we can get to Heaven by being "good," and we don't think anybody really goes to Hell - except maybe Hitler and Stalin. We fail to recognize that we are all lost, every one of us, until Jesus Christ's blood washes us clean.

One of the questions we might want to ask is whether our churches have fallen into a worldly mentality toward sin. Do our churches recognize the world is filled with lost people destined for Hell without Jesus Christ? Do our churches offer us salvation through Jesus Christ alone - the good news that God loves us and sent Christ to die for us? We need to speak the truth in love, or people will die with no appreciation for their true predicament. We cannot preach the user friendly message of "You're okay. I'm okay." We need to say, "Hey! We're all in trouble! The earth is falling out from under us and we're all going to die! But good news! God has made a bridge to the other side of the canyon! Take it!"

We are a lukewarm culture, and for too long we've allowed the world to tell us what to think. We need to be fire-hot Christians, filled with true, longsuffering and devoted love for our fellow humans. If we open ourselves to the guidance of His Word and His love through His Spirit, I think we'll be astounded where the Lord takes us.

Chapter 12

The Churches: A Summary

We've gone through all the churches, and we covered a great many ideas. Let's review them. First, in the words Jesus speaks to each church, He offers admonitions that should be taken seriously by all the churches:

Admonitory Application

Ephesus	Remember devotion, not just doctrine.
Smyrna	Endure persecution.
Pergamos	Purify ambassadors.
Thyatira	Reject pagan practices.
Sardis	Keep watchful and diligent.
Philadelphia	Engage in missionary outreach.
Laodicea	Reject compromise.

Both Smyrna and Philadelphia have no criticism, and both of these cities remain today. Let's remember that each of the churches had a different perception of themselves than the Lord Himself had. How sobering to us in our own conceits.

Personal Application

Each of the churches have a personal application, one that we ourselves can take to heart.

Ephesus	Make right priorities. Love Christ first.
Smyrna	Withstand Satanic opposition.
Pergamos	Avoid spiritual compromise.
Thyatira	Reject pagan Practices.
Sardis	Keep watchful and diligent.
Philadelphia	Continue loyal ambassadorship.
Laodicea	Avoid materialistic apostasy.

Overcomer's Promises

We can also remember that God has wonderful things planned for us. Our job is to keep trusting Him and following Him. He's going to give us the world! It will all be over one day, and we'll get to be with Him forever. We need to keep at it patiently until then.

Ephesus	Eat of Tree of Life.
Smyrna	Not hurt of second death.
Pergamos	Manna, white stone, new name.
Thyatira	Power over nations.
Sardis	Walk with Him in white; name not blotted out, confessed before all heaven
Philadelphia	Pillar in Temple, name of God, name of His city, His new name.
Laodicea	Sit with Him on His throne.

Prophetic Church Period

If these seven churches represent times in the history of the Church Age, then we are in the age of the church of Laodicea. I'm convinced of it. That gives us a kick that says we need to stop depending on our riches and truly depend on Christ Jesus, but it also tells us Jesus Christ is returning soon. That's exciting! Let's keep diligent at the work He's given us until He comes!

Ephesus	First 100 years of Church
Smyrna	Early Persecution (A.D. 100-313)
Pergamos	Imperial Church (A.D. 313-590)
Thyatira	Papal Rule (590 - Tribulation)
Sardis	Denominational Churches (1517 - Tribulation)
Philadelphia	Missionary Church (1730 - Rapture)
Laodicea	Modern Apostate Church

We are in the age in which the Church thinks it's wealthy. We have big fancy cathedrals, yet it can be hard to hear the true Gospel of Jesus Christ. We find many churches today that will declare that Jesus was a great teacher and a fine moral example. Many will even admit that Jesus performed miracles. A range of churches today, however, fail to declare Christ's shed blood as the only remedy for our sin.

Jesus declared that the two great commandments are to love God with all our hearts and to love our neighbors as ourselves.[46] 1 Corinthians 13 tells us what love looks like. Love is patient and kind. It's not proud or unseemly or easily provoked. Love keeps no record of wrongs and it isn't quick to assume evil of the beloved. But love also rejoices in the truth. Love *requires* us to speak the truth. Of course, we must do so with the wisdom and guidance of the Holy Spirit, in the love of God, or we're just noisy gongs and cymbals.[47]

Unfortunately, our culture is filled with people who no longer believe that *truth* is something real, and the church of Laodicea in our midst cares more about popular opinion than it cares about whether people might be in eternal danger.

Biblical Christianity is not all-inclusive. It's not particularly tolerant, because it insists that Jesus Christ is the only way to God. All paths do not reach the top of the mountain. Jesus said in John 14:6, "*I am the way, the truth, and the life: no man cometh unto the Father, but by me.*" Biblical Christianity does not leave a lot of wiggle room for other belief systems there, and that puts some people off. Rather than reaching out to lost people, however, the Laodicean churches throw out the very heart of the Gospel.

John 3:16 tells us that God so loved the world that He gave His only Son, and 2 Peter 3:9 tells us that God is not willing that any should perish. In the Gospels, Jesus ate with prostitutes and tax collectors - sinners - and their lives were changed. The Lord God of eternity sent His Son to save us, but Jesus also sweated blood in the Garden of Gethsemane, asking His Father to find another way if it were possible.[48] There was no other way. Jesus' death is the only way. That may be restrictive, but it also happens to be the situation we're all in.

> *Enter ye in at the strait gate: for wide is the gate, and broad is the way, that leadeth to destruction, and many there be which go in thereat: Because strait is the gate, and narrow is the way, which leadeth unto life, and few there be that find it.*
>
> Matthew 7:13-14

Chapter 13

Seven Kingdom Parables

As we near the end of this little study, I want to share another passage that I usually associate with these seven churches. I won't take the time to go through it in detail - that's something I hope you do on your own. However, I do want to give a quick profile.

In Matthew 13, Jesus gives His disciples seven parables. These are sometimes called the "kingdom parables" because Jesus repeatedly says, "the kingdom of heaven is like unto…" at the beginning of these.

The first nine verses of Matthew 13 tell about the sower who goes out to sow seed. It's a familiar parable. Some of the seed falls on the hard path, some falls among thorns and some in rocky soil. The seed is carried off the path by birds, or it sprouts up and then dies in the rocky and thorny soil. Only in the good soil does it grow to produce fruit. Jesus explains to His disciples that the seed is the Word of God, and the soils are the hearts of those who hear it. This is a parable many of us learned in Sunday school as little children.

After this longer parable, we find a series of others. Next, we find a parable that is about how

Satan sewed tares in the wheat field. God tells the angels to let the wheat grow, then collect the tares first and burn them before gathering the wheat into barns.

The next parable is about the mustard seed, which is a tiny seed that grows into a large tree. The parable after that is about a woman who hides leaven in three measures of wheat until it's all leavened. There's an explanatory break, and then we finish with three last parables. A man finds a treasure in a field, and he sells all he has to buy the field. The next is similar; a man finds a pearl of great price, and he sells all he has to buy it. Finally, we find the drag net that catches all kinds of fish, but then the fishermen go through and keep the good fish and toss out the bad.

There's a little proverb after these that some regard as an eighth parable, but it's really just a proverb. All told, there are seven of these kingdom parables:

#	Verses	Kingdom Parable
1.	3-9	Sower & 4 Soils
	10-17	-Why Parables?
	18-23	-Sower & 4 Soils Explained
2.	24-30	Tares & Wheat
3.	31-32	Mustard Seed
4.	33	Woman & Leaven
	34-35	-Why Parables?
	36-43	-Tares & Wheat Explained
5.	44	Treasure in the Field
6.	45-46	Pearl of Great Price
7.	46-50	Dragnet in the sea

As we study through Matthew 13, we find two small sections that explain why Jesus teaches in parables. He makes a strange remark. He points out that these parables are not to illuminate, but to hide. Most people think parables are given because they're teaching aids. They can be if we understand the meaning of them, but Jesus points out that only His insiders will understand them.

We find another interesting statement in Matthew 13:35. Matthew tells us it was prophesied that Jesus would speak in parables and, "utter things which have been kept secret from the foundation of the world." It appears the truths of these parables aren't found in the Old Testament, because they've been hidden since the foundation of the world.

In Ephesians 3:3-6, Paul explains that the salvation of the Gentiles, the Church, was a mystery not understood in former ages. It was a recent revelation by the Spirit. The Church as the body of Christ is a mystery.

I believe that these seven kingdom parables are offering illuminating information about the Church. Consider the woman and the leaven, the fourth parable here:

> *Another parable spake he unto them;*
> *The kingdom of heaven is like unto*
> *leaven, which a woman took, and hid in*
> *three measures of meal, till the whole was*
> *leavened.*

Matthew 13:33

What does that mean? Jesus doesn't explain it for us as He did the tares and the wheat.

We have to remember something important as we try to work these out: Jesus was a Jewish rabbi speaking to Jewish disciples. We need to remember what leaven represented to the Jews. Leaven is always a type of sin, because sin corrupts by puffing us up. The root of sin was Satan's pride. At Passover, the Jews spend time removing all the leaven from their houses. In Matthew 16:6, Jesus tells the disciples to beware the leaven of the Pharisees and the Sadducees. Leaven is consistently correlated with sin.

Three measure of meal is a fellowship offering to a Jew or an Arab. This goes back to Genesis 18, when the LORD and two angels visited Abraham by the oaks of Mamre. In verse 6, Abraham tells Sarah to quickly take three measures of meal and bake cakes on the hearth for them to eat. Abraham goes and gets a tender calf and sets meat before the three visitors, along with the cakes and butter and milk. After that time, three measures of meal became symbolic for a fellowship offering.

With this background, it would make Jews gasp to hear Jesus tell that a woman had put leaven into three measures of meal. That shouldn't be done. Yet, consider the fourth letter of the seven churches, the letter to Thyatira. Who is leading the people astray? Jezebel. How is she leading them astray? False doctrine - teaching them to sin. Wow. There seems to be a strong parallel there.

#	Verses	Kingdom Parable	Church
1.	3-9	Sower & 4 Soils	Ephesus
2.	24-30	Tares & Wheat	Smyrna
3.	31-32	Mustard Seed	Pergamos
4.	33	Woman & Leaven	Thyatira
5.	44	Treasure in the Field	Sardis
6.	45-46	Pearl of Great Price	Philadelphia
7.	46-50	Dragnet in the sea	Laodicea

Remember the line common to all the churches? "He that hath an ear, let him hear." We also find this statement twice in Matthew 13: "Who hath ears to hear, let him hear." The seven kingdom parables seem to fit the seven churches. The sower and the four soils are Ephesus, which had been distracted from its first love.

The church of Smyrna had to deal with the blasphemy of those who said they were Jews but were not, which is like the tares and the wheat in the second parable. Tares were the *zizania* - a poisonous seed in Israel that looks just like wheat while it is growing. It's not until it matures that it turns black so that it can be separated from the wheat and burned.

Consider the third parable about the mustard seed and its parallel in Pergamos.

Another parable put he forth unto them, saying, The kingdom of heaven is like to a grain of mustard seed, which a man took, and sowed in his field: Which indeed is the least of all seeds: but when it is grown, it is the greatest among herbs, and becometh a

*tree, so that the birds of the air come and
lodge in the branches thereof.*

Matthew 13:31-32

If we go to Israel, we discover that mustard
grows as yellow flowers along the road. Mustard
seeds grow to plants only about three or four feet
high. Have you ever seen a bird lodged in a branch
three feet high? No. This is a strange mustard
tree on which the birds of the air can rest. It's a
monstrosity, and it's grown in such a way that birds
can roost in its branches.

Return to the first parable. What were the
birds? They were ministers of Satan. Wait a minute,
what's going on here? Let's compare this parable
to Pergamos. These were Christians surviving even
under Satan's throne, and the church had some
good things about it, but it also had those who
committed fornication and ate food sacrificed to
idols. Its intended purpose was a lovely yellow
herb, but when the Rome took over the church,
it grew into a monstrosity that allowed the evils
of paganism to roost in its branches.

How does Sardis fit, then? This parable
describes a man who found a treasure in the field,
and he sold all he had to buy it. Sardis didn't give
up all it had for Christ. In fact, it was dead while
it looked alive. But, Sardis isn't the buyer. Sardis is
the treasure. The One that gave up all that He had
for the sake of the treasure is Jesus Christ! He didn't
buy just one little parcel, He bought the whole
field. He died on the cross for the entire world,

for all sinners. Who is the treasure hidden in the field? That's Sardis, the sardonyx. It's you and me.

The next parable describes a man who sells all He has for a pearl of great price. Again, Jesus is doing the buying. The problem with a pearl is that oysters are not kosher. Pearls were prized by the Gentiles, not by Jews. The Church is a gentile organism, though, so that makes sense. Like a pearl, the Church starts by implanting an irritation that develops into something beautiful. After it is removed from its place of growth, it can become an item of adornment.

The church at Philadelphia was the gentile church that was beautiful, created by struggles. It won't see the great Tribulation; it's removed in the Rapture. That's wild stuff.

Laodicea is the dragnet that catches everything, but in the end, the Lord will separate the sheep from the goats.

I've only briefly touched on this idea here. We would need to go into a little more depth to see the full fit of each of these, and I recommend digging into it as an interesting topic of study. I can see the match between the seven churches and kingdom parables, but you might disagree with me. That's fine, but I believe it still makes a valuable study.

I find fascinating the various parallels between these seven kingdom parables of Matthew 13 and the seven churches of Revelation 2-3. If I'm correct to connect these two passages, it shouldn't be a surprise because they both have the same author. Jesus gave His disciples the seven kingdom parables, and He dictated the seven letters to the churches.

Chapter 14

The Seven Letters and Us

The most important aspect of this study, of course, is how these letters apply to us today. We can look more closely at the history of each church in its own time, and we can see the parallels between the letters and the various periods of Church history. However, the most important part of reading these letters is what we can take to heart personally. Seven times Jesus said, "He that hath an ear, let him hear what the Spirit saith unto the churches." We all have ears.

We all love to identify with the church of Philadelphia. However, I'm certain there's some Ephesus in all of us. We can all get a little too concerned with doctrine and with the work of doing church and forget to love our Lord as the whole purpose of it. We get too busy in the service of the King to take time for just enjoying the King.

There are those who can identify with Smyrna in the world today. There are plenty of Christians being severely persecuted because they are faithful to the Word of God. Few of us in the West are among them. We might have coworkers raise their eyebrows or call us "crazy" when we tell about what God is doing in our lives, but we're free to say what we think without fear for our lives. Our pastors are not being dragged off and murdered. We don't face constant church bombings or church shootings or midnight interrogations. The ministry Open Doors USA reports that in 2015, Nigerian Christians suffered 198 different church attacks, and 4,028 people were killed.[49] In North Korea, Somalia, Afghanistan, Pakistan, Sudan, Syria, Iraq and Iran Christians are targeted on a regular basis. They are suffering and they need our prayers and support. The church of Smyrna is having victories today, and we can participate in those victories through prayer and physical aid.

We might not like to admit it, but we can be Pergamos. We can be Sardis and Laodicea. We can look at our own church homes, our own families, our own lives and see our own inclinations to worship things other than Jesus. We can look at our own hearts and recognize when we've cared more about looking good than being full of Christ's life through the Holy Spirit. It's easy to be lukewarm when we're comfortable and have a fridge full of food and every material convenience. The problem isn't poverty or prosperity. The real issue is one of the heart. Where are our treasures? Are they in heaven, or are they sitting in our driveway?

There may be a time when we in America have to face persecution. Our country is greatly divided, and people who serve Christ faithfully are no longer honored. Those who hate our Lord are shouting louder and louder, and too many Christians are just sitting around watching movies. Unless things change in this country - unless we throw off our tendencies to be Sardis and Laodicea - we could be in a lot of trouble. Blessed is that nation whose God is the Lord.

As we go to work each day, as we spend time with our friends and families, we represent Jesus Christ. We can't merely give Christ a few hours on Sunday morning. We need to be on our knees for our families and our neighbors. James 5:16 tells us, *"The effectual fervent prayer of a righteous man availeth much."*

In that same verse, James tells us to confess our faults to one another and to pray for one another, that we may be healed. We need to be gathering together in small groups and praying for one another. We need people we can confide in - and we need to be safe people for others to confide in. We need that. We need to be bound together in love. Nothing is better than brothers and sisters joining together in a fellowship of true kindness and patience and a desire to help one another. Nothing is better.

We are in a spiritual battle. If Satan can get us to just sit on the sidelines doing nothing, then he can take ground - and that ground means hearts and lives. We may be entering into a very difficult period, and we need to be fighting spiritually for those around us.

We are not earth-dwellers. We are just passing through.

I've seen many churches across America that are wonderful Bible teaching churches. They really have it all together in every way - but many of them still do not have a common burden with the other pastors in their area. They're still building their own turf.

I would recommend that the pastors of Bible-loving churches gather together with other pastors in their area. There's a growing movement for this, and it's greatly needed. Pastors are gathering together and praying together for their communities, and I think that's exciting. Denominationalism built a barrier that has made many churches tragically insular. We do not want to compromise the Gospel of Christ, of course, but where we have a Bible-based view together, small differences can be set aside with an agreement to disagree. Pastors need to gather and pray together. I think that's important. Pastors need to be able to confess their sins one to another and have people they can trust to pray with them - just like the rest of us.

God has given us an incredible gift. He gave us His Son - that's the most important thing. He has also given us His Spirit, and by His Spirit we can do all that God asks us to do. Not by might nor by power, but by His Spirit. We simply need to fall at the knees of our Savior who loves us so much and seek His help and guidance every day.

Father we praise You for these seven letters. Thank You for Your Word and its timeliness. Father, we pray that through Your Spirit, You would help each of us to hear what You have to say to all seven churches. We pray that You would search our hearts and reveal to each of us our secret sins, that we might hand them over and walk ever closer with You. We suspect that we are in for some surprises on our report cards, just like these seven churches. Please help us understand Your heart for us, show us how to repair those areas where we need repentance. Give us a perspective of where we stand and what work lies ahead for us, that we might be diligent stewards of your resources and be effective husbandmen of your vineyard. You have given us everything, Father. You have sacrificed Your Son for us. We long to give our lives back to You, to give You what You desire in us. Father, we commit ourselves before Your throne, in the name of our Lord and Savior, Jesus Christ. Amen.

Endnotes

1   Isaiah 6, Ezekiel 1 & 10.

2   Irenaeus (A.D. 175-185). *Against Heresies*, 5.30.3.

3   Eusebius (340). *Ecclesiastical History*, 3.23.

4   See 2 Timothy 2:15

5   Pliny the Elder (A.D. 7-79) *Natural History* 36.21.95.

6   *Ibid.*

7   Acts 20:31

8   Acts 19:28, 34

9   Acts 20:23

10 Matthew 11:15; 13:9, 43; Mark 4:9, 23; 7:16; Luke 8:8; 14:35

11 Schaff, P., trans. (1902). *Codex Justinianus*, Lib 3, Tit 12.3; in *History of the Christian Church, Vol. 3* (5th ed.; p. 380). New York: Scribner.

12 Tertullian, (A.D. 197). *Apologeticus*, Ch. 50.

13 Cf. Deuteronomy 9:4-5

14 Joshua 5:12

15 1 Kings 18:19

16 Exodus 34:13; Deuteronomy 7:5, 12:3

17 Jeremiah 7:18; 44:17-19, 25

18 Jeremiah 44:27

19 Hunt, D. (1994). *A Woman Rides the Beast*. Eugene, Oregon: Harvest House.

20 Isaiah 11:1-4

21 Matthew 23:8-10

22   Eusebius (340). *Ecclesiastical History.* 2.25.5-8.

23   John 21:15-17

24   Chamberlin, E.R. (1969). *The Bad Popes* (pg. 27).
     New York: Barnes & Noble Books.

25   Gibbon, E. (1881). *The History of the Decline and Fall
     of the Roman Empire, Volume 2* (pg. 240). New York:
     Phillips and Hunt.

26   Ibid, 240-241.

27   Pope Victor III (1086-1087). *Dialogues*, Book iii.

28   Platina, B. (1479) *Lives of the Popes*, 2.276

29   Habakkuk 2:4; Romans 3:25; Ephesians 1:7; 2:8-9;
     Galatians 3:11; Hebrews 9:12-14; 10:38-39;
     1 John 1:7-9; Revelation 1:5

30   John 3:3-8; Titus 3:5-6

31   John 10:7b-8a

32   2 Timothy 4:8

33   Isaiah 57:15; Acts 2:27, 3:14; Revelation 6:10

34   Jeremiah 10:10; John 14:6; 2 Corinthians 1:18-20;
     1 John 5:20

35   Acts 8:3, 9:1-2, 22:3-5

36   1 Thessalonians 4:17

37   Mark 9:35, 10:31

38   Luke 14:7-11

39   1 Kings 7:21

40   Tacitus (A.D. 109). *Annals* 14:27

41   Colossians 1:7 - Philemon 1:23 confirms that
     Epaphras had also become Paul's fellow prisoner.

42   Colossians 4:12-14

43 Colossians 4:16

44 Psalm 2:12, 110; John 1:1-3; Colossians 1:15-17; Hebrews 1:2

45 Hebrews 4:14-16

46 Matthew 22:37-40

47 1 Corinthians 13:1-2

48 Matthew 26:39-42; Luke 22:41-45

49 Janelle P (March 1, 2016). Killing of Christians in Nigeria Has Increased by 62%. Open Doors USA, https://www.opendoorsusa.org

About the Author

Chuck Missler
Founder, Koinonia House

Chuck Missler was raised in Southern California.

Chuck demonstrated an aptitude for technical interests as a youth. He became a ham radio operator at age nine and started piloting airplanes as a teenager. While still in high school, Chuck built a digital computer in the family garage.

His plans to pursue a doctorate in electrical engineering at Stanford University were interrupted when he received a Congressional appointment to the United States Naval Academy at Annapolis. Graduating with honors, Chuck took his commission in the Air Force. After completing flight training, he met and married Nancy (who later founded The King's High Way ministry). Chuck joined the Missile Program and eventually became Branch Chief of the Department of Guided Missiles.

Chuck made the transition from the military to the private sector when he became a systems engineer with TRW, a large aerospace firm. He then went on to serve as a senior analyst with a non-profit think tank where he conducted projects for the intelligence community and the Department of Defense. During that time, Chuck earned a master's degree in engineering at UCLA, supplementing previous graduate work in applied mathematics, advanced statistics and information sciences.

Recruited into senior management at the Ford Motor Company in Dearborn, Michigan, Chuck established the first international computer network in 1966. He left Ford to start his own company, a computer network firm that was subsequently acquired by Automatic Data Processing (listed on the New York Stock Exchange) to become its Network Services Division.

As Chuck notes, his day of reckoning came in the early '90s when — as the result of a merger — he found himself the chairman and a major shareholder of a small, publicly owned development company known as Phoenix Group International. The firm established an $8 billion joint venture with the Soviet Union to supply personal computers to their 143,000 schools. Due to several unforeseen circumstances, the venture failed. The Misslers lost everything, including their home, automobiles and insurance.

It was during this difficult time that Chuck turned to God and the Bible. As a child he had developed an intense interest in the Bible; studying it became a favorite pastime. In the 1970s, while still in the corporate world, Chuck began leading weekly Bible studies at the 30,000 member Calvary Chapel Costa Mesa, in California. He and Nancy established Koinonia House in 1973, an organization devoted to encouraging people to study the Bible.

Chuck had enjoyed a longtime, personal relationship with Hal Lindsey, who upon hearing of Chuck's professional misfortune, convinced him that he could easily succeed as an independent author and speaker. Over the years, Chuck had developed a loyal following. (Through Doug Wetmore, head of the tape ministry of Firefighters for Christ, Chuck learned that over 7 million copies of his taped Bible studies were scattered throughout the world.) Koinonia House then became Chuck's full-time profession.

Learn the Bible

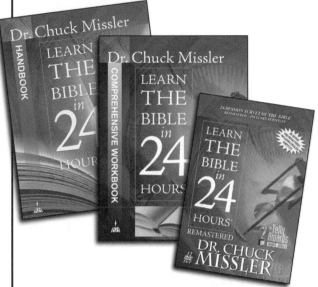

Are you ready for a detailed yet thoroughly enjoyable study of the most profound book ever written?

Using sound scientific facts, historical analysis, and Biblical narrative, acclaimed teacher Dr. Chuck Missler weaves together a rich tapestry of information—providing an accurate understanding of Scripture's relation to itself, to us, and to the world at large.

Examine the heroic tales of Exodus, the lasting wisdom of Proverbs, or even the enigmatic imagery of Revelation with the simple, Scripturally sound insights and fresh perspectives found in *Learn the Bible in 24 Hours*. Whether you want to explore some of the less-discussed nuances of Scripture or you need a comprehensive refresher course on the Bible's themes and stories, *Learn the Bible in 24 Hours* is a great guide.

How We Got Our Bible

- Where did our Bible come from? How good are the texts?
- Why do we believe its origin is supernatural?
- How do we know that it really is the Word of God?
- How accurate are our translations?
- Which version is the best?

Chuck Missler, an internationally recognized Biblical authority, reviews the origin of both the Old and New Testaments in light of recent discoveries and controversies.